COLLINS

Cycling *in* DORSET & HAMPSHIRE

HarperCollins*Publishers*

Published by Collins
An imprint of HarperCollins*Publishers*
77-85 Fulham Palace Road
London W6 8JB

First published 1998

Routes compiled by Jim Deeley, Keith and Janet Matthews, John and Mary Burrows, John Darby, Peter Loakes, George May and Kevin Wright.
Design by Creative Matters Design Consultancy, Glasgow.
Typeset by Bob Vickers.

Photographs reproduced by kind permission of the following:
International Photobank pages 5, 11, 25, 37, 45, 53, 85, 101, 104, 110; Keith Matthews pages 61, 65; Andy Williams pages 8, 17, 23, 27, 33, 35, 41, 69, 73, 77, 81, 107.

The landscape is changing all the time. While every care has been taken in the preparation of this guide, the Publisher accepts no responsibility whatsoever for any loss, damage, injury or inconvenience sustained or caused as a result of using this guide.

Printed in Italy

ISBN 0 00 448682 X
98/1/14

CONTENTS

KEY TO ROUTES

Route colour coding

undemanding rides compiled specifically with families in mind
15-25km (10-15 miles)

middle distance rides suitable for all cyclists
25-40km (15-25 miles)

half-day rides for the more experienced and adventurous cyclist
40-60km (25-40 miles)

challenging full-day rides
over 60km (over 40 miles)

grande randonnée – a grand cycling tour
100km (60 miles)

Routes marked with this symbol are off-road or have off-road sections
(includes well-surfaced cycleways as well as rougher off-road tracks)

View from the Foreland, Studland (see Route 15)

LOCATION MAP

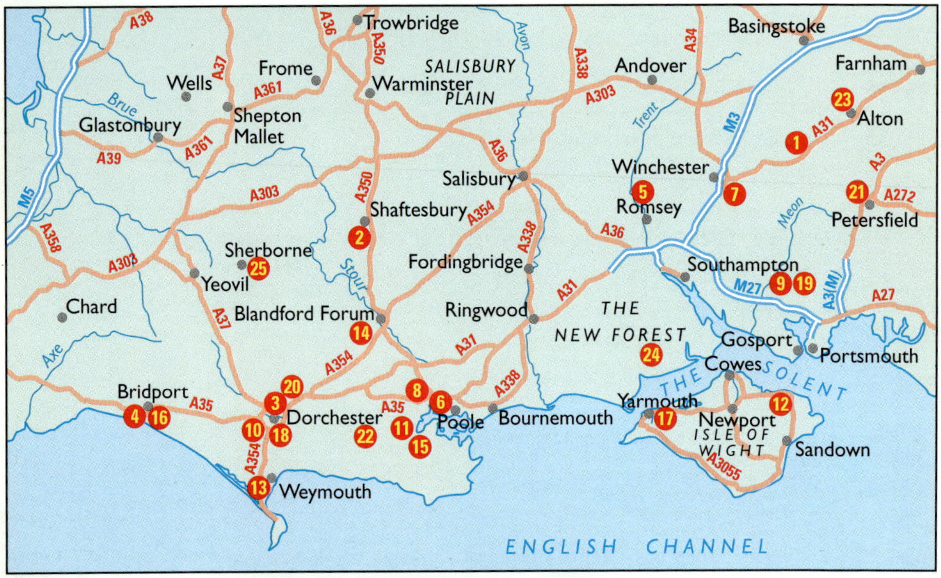

Trowbridge
Basingstoke
Frome
Wells
Warminster
SALISBURY PLAIN
Andover
Farnham
Alton
Glastonbury
Shepton Mallet
Salisbury
Winchester
Shaftesbury
Romsey
Petersfield
Sherborne
Yeovil
Fordingbridge
Southampton
Chard
Blandford Forum
Ringwood
THE NEW FOREST
Gosport
Portsmouth
Cowes
THE SOLENT
Bridport
Dorchester
Poole
Bournemouth
Yarmouth
Newport
ISLE OF WIGHT
Sandown
Weymouth
ENGLISH CHANNEL
M5 M3 M27 A3(M) A38 A37 A361 A39 A303 A358 A36 A350 A354 A338 A31 A34 A3 A272 A27 A35 A3055
Brue Avon Trent Stour Meon Axe
1 2 3 4 5 6 7 8 9 10 11 12 13 14 15 16 17 18 19 20 21 22 23 24 25

KEY TO ROUTE MAPS

M23	Motorway
A259	'A' road / Dual carriageway
B2130	'B' road / Dual carriageway
	Good minor road
	Minor road
	Track / bridleway
	Railway / station
	Canal / river
	Lake
50	Contour (height in metres)
	Urban area
	Woodland

	Cycle route
	Optional route
	Start of cycle route
12	Route direction
B	Place of interest
	Public house
	Café / refreshments
	Restaurant
	Convenience store

P	Parking
	Telephone
	Picnic site
	Camping site
	Public toilets
	Viewpoint
	Place of worship
	Golf course
	Tumulus

Height above sea level

50	100	150	200	300 metres
165	330	490	655	980 feet

INTRODUCTION

How to use this guide

Collins' *Cycling in Dorset and Hampshire* has been devised for all those who want trips out on their bicycles along quiet roads and tracks, passing interesting places and convenient refreshment stops without having to devise their own routes. Each of the 25 routes in this book has been compiled and ridden by an experienced cyclist for cyclists of all abilities.

Cycling in Dorset and Hampshire is easy to use. Routes range from undemanding rides compiled specifically with families in mind to challenging full-day rides; the type of route is easily identified by colour coding (see page 5). At the start of each route an information box summarises: total distance (in kilometres/miles – distances have been rounded up or down throughout to the nearest 0.5km/mile and are approximate only); grade (easy, moderate or strenuous based on distance and difficulty); terrain; an average time to allow for the route; directions to the start of the route by car and, if appropriate, by train.

Each route is fully mapped and has concise, easy-to-follow directions. Comprehensive information on places of interest and convenient refreshment stops along each route are also given. Accumulated mileages within each route description give an indication of progress, while the profile diagram is a graphic representation of gradients along the route. These should be used as a guide only.

The following abbreviations are used in the route directions:

LHF	left hand fork
RHF	right hand fork
SO	straight on
SP	signpost
TJ	T junction
TL	turn left
TR	turn right
XR	crossroads

Cycling in Dorset and Hampshire

The rides in this book run through Dorset, west Hampshire (including the New Forest) and the Isle of Wight – areas of beautiful countryside and dramatic coastline.

The routes are designed to stay away from busy main roads as much as possible and to allow cyclists to discover the peaceful back lanes, bridleways and cycleways that cross the country, passing all manner of museums, castles, historic houses and other attractions. Although the major roads are busy, particularly in summer, the back lanes have remarkably little traffic. The areas covered by these routes are still predominantly rural – many of the towns and villages have preserved their traditional character which you will see along the way.

Parts of Hampshire and much of Dorset are hilly, and there are steep sections to be tackled in some of the routes. However, the effort is compensated for by the spectacular views – and you can always get off and push your bike!

Geology, geography and history

Dorset's geology comprises layers of limestone, clay, chalk and, topmost, sands and gravels. Subsequent erosion has given Dorset its dramatic coastline. The landscape is littered with ancient tumuli and earthworks. By 500 BC much of the area was held by the Durotriges tribe, who built impressive hillforts such as that at Maiden Castle. Conquered by the Romans, Maiden Castle was abandoned in favour of a new town, Durnovaria, which became Dorchester, Thomas Hardy's Casterbridge. Together with its long history, later influences have shaped Dorset. Lyme Regis and Weymouth became fashionable resorts during the 18th century, followed by Swanage and Bournemouth in the 19th century, encouraging the development of railways into the area. Many disused railway tracks have now been transformed into traffic-free trails for cyclists and walkers. Since World War I, the army has used large areas of heathland for tank training. This has preserved the landscape from modern farming methods, although extensive conifer plantations, introduced in the 1920s, have resulted in the loss of large areas of heath and grassland. Dorset remains predominantly rural and you can still see the market towns, villages and countryside that inspired so much of Thomas Hardy's writing.

Hampshire closely mirrors Dorset – chalk downs, rolling hills and heathland. There are large numbers of prehistoric remains and earthworks, evidence of Roman occupation, Norman and medieval castles, manors and churches. However, because of its proximity to London and ease of access, Hampshire has developed differently. There has been heavy

View of Durdle Door (see Route 18)

urbanisation along the coast and motorways cross the countryside. But despite this, there are still hidden places to discover and explore.

The New Forest, named by William the Conqueror in the 11th century, was set aside as his private deer hunting ground. At that time the land was mostly gorse and heath, but during the 14th century woodlands were established and the area became increasingly important for timber production. Supplies of wood for shipbuilding were sent to dockyards in Portsmouth and at Bucklers Hard. At various times, areas of the forest have been replanted. Today the forest is composed of the relics of the ancient woodland, more recent coniferous forest and large areas of open heath and grassland.

Old Stone Age tools dating back to circa 80,000 BC have been found on the Isle of Wight, which was probably part of the mainland until around 4000 BC. The island's agricultural prosperity and strategic position made it vulnerable to attack – from the Romans, Saxons, Jutes, Norsemen and Normans. Smuggling was a major industry, involving whole communities. When duties were reduced on many goods in the early 19th century, agriculture and tourism took over, leaving the island a pleasant, unspoilt place with the added fun of a sea crossing over the Solent.

Preparing for a cycling trip

Basic maintenance

A cycle ride is an immense pleasure, particularly on a warm sunny day. Nothing is better than coasting along a country lane gazing over the countryside. Unfortunately, not every cycling day is as perfect as this, and it is important to make sure that your bike is in good order and that you are taking the necessary clothing and supplies with you.

Before you go out on your bicycle check that everything is in order. Pump the tyres up if needed, and check that the brakes are working properly and that nothing is loose – the brakes are the only means of stopping quickly and safely. If there is a problem and you are not sure that you can fix it, take the bike to a cycle repair shop – they can often deal with small repairs very quickly.

When you go out cycling it is important to take either a puncture repair kit or a spare inner tube – it is often quicker to replace the inner tube in the event of a puncture, though it may be a good idea to practise first. You also need a pump, and with a slow puncture the pump may be enough to get you home. To remove the tyre you need a set of tyre levers. Other basic tools are an Allen key and a spanner. Some wheels on modern bikes can be removed by quick release levers built into the bike. Take a lock for your bike and if you have to leave it at any time, leave it in public view and locked through the frame and front wheel to something secure.

What to wear and take with you

It is not necessary to buy specialised cycling clothes. If it is not warm enough to wear shorts wear trousers which are easy to move in but fairly close to the leg below the knee – leggings are ideal – as this stops the trousers catching the chain. If you haven't got narrow-legged trousers, bicycle clips will hold them in. Jeans are not a good idea as they are rather tight and difficult to cycle in, and if they get wet they take a long time to dry. If your shorts or trousers are thin you might get a bit sore from being too long on the saddle. This problem can be reduced by using a gel saddle, and by wearing thicker, or extra, pants. Once you are a committed cyclist you can buy cycling shorts; or undershorts which have a protective pad built in and which can be worn under anything. It is a good idea to wear several thin layers of clothes so that you can add or remove layers as necessary. A zip-fronted top gives easy temperature control. Make sure you have something warm and something waterproof.

If you wear shoes with a firm, flat sole you will be able to exert pressure on the pedals easily, and will have less work to do to make the bicycle move. Gloves not only keep your hands warm but protect them in the event that you come off, and cycling mittens which cushion your hands are not expensive. A helmet is not a legal requirement, but it will protect your head if you fall.

In general it is a good idea to wear bright clothing so that you can be easily seen by motorists, and this is particularly important when it is overcast or getting dark. If you might be out in the dark or twilight fit your bicycle with lights – by law your bicycle must have a reflector. You can also buy reflective bands for your ankles, or to wear over your shoulder and back, and these help motorists to see you.

You may be surprised how quickly you use up energy when cycling, and it is important to eat a carbohydrate meal before you set out. When planning a long ride, eat well the night before. You should eat small amounts of food regularly while you are cycling, or you may find that your energy suddenly disappears, particularly if there are hills or if the weather is cold. It is important to always carry something to eat with you – chocolate, bananas, biscuits – so that if you do start fading away you can restore yourself quickly. In warm weather you will sweat and use up fluid, and you always need to carry something to drink – water will do! Many bicycles have a fitment in which to put a water bottle, and if you don't have one a cycle shop should be able to fit one.

It is also a good idea to carry a small first aid kit. This should include elastoplasts or bandages, sunburn cream, and an anti-histamine in case you are stung by a passing insect.

It is a good idea to have a pannier to carry all these items. Some fit on the handlebars, some to the back of the seat and some onto a back rack. For a day's ride you probably won't need a lot of carrying capacity, but it is better to carry items in a pannier rather than in a rucksack on your back. Pack items that you are carrying carefully – loose items can be dangerous.

Getting to the start of the ride

If you are lucky you will be able to cycle to the start of the ride, but often transport is necessary. If you travel there by train, some sprinter services carry two bicycles without prior booking. Other services carry bicycles free in off-peak periods, but check the details with your local station. Alternatively, you could use your car – it may be possible to get a bike in the back of a hatchback if you take out the front wheel. There are inexpensive, easily fitted car racks which carry bicycles safely. Your local cycle store will be able to supply one to suit you.

Cycling on-road

Cycling on back roads is a delight with quiet lanes, interesting villages, good views and a smooth easy surface to coast along on. The cycle rides in this book are mainly on quiet roads but you sometimes cross busy roads or have stretches on B roads, and whatever sort of road you are on it is essential to ride safely. Always be aware of the possibility or existence of other traffic. Glance behind regularly, signal before you turn or change lane, and keep to the left. If there are motorists around, make sure that they have seen you before you cross their path. Cycling can be dangerous if you are competing for space with motor vehicles, many of which seem to have difficulty in seeing cyclists. When drivers are coming out of side

Thomas Hardy's cottage (see Route 22)

roads, catch their eye before you ride in front of them.

You will find that many roads have potholes and uneven edges. They are much more difficult to spot when you are in a group because of the restricted view ahead, and therefore warnings need to be given. It is a good idea to cycle about a metre out into the road, conditions permitting, so that you avoid the worst of the uneven surfaces and to give you room to move in to the left if you are closely overtaken by a motor vehicle.

Other things to be careful of are slippery roads, particularly where there is mud or fallen leaves. Sudden rain after a period of dry weather often makes the roads extremely slippery. Dogs, too, are a hazard because they often move unpredictably, and sometimes like to chase cyclists. If you are not happy, stop or go slowly until the problem has passed.

Pedalling

Many modern bikes have 18 or 21 gears with three rings at the front and six or seven on the back wheel, and for much of the time you will find that the middle gear at the front with the range of gears at the back will be fine. Use your gears to find one that is easy to pedal along in so that your feet move round easily and you do not put too much pressure on your knees. If you are new to the bike and the gears it is a good idea to practise changing the gears on a stretch of flat, quiet road so that when you need to change gears quickly you will be ready to do so.

Cycling in a group

When cycling in a group it is essential to do so in a disciplined manner for your own, and others', safety. Do not ride too close to the bicycle in front of you – keep about a bicycle's length between you so that you will have space to brake or stop. Always keep both hands on the handlebars, except when signalling, etc. It is alright to cycle two abreast on quiet roads, but if it is necessary to change from cycling two abreast to single file this is usually done by the outside rider falling in behind the nearside rider; always cycle in single file where there are double white lines, on busy roads, or on narrow and winding roads where you have a restricted view of the road ahead. Overtake on the right (outside) only; do not overtake on the inside.

It is important to pass information to other members of the group, for example:

car up – a vehicle is coming up behind the group and will be overtaking;

car down – a vehicle is coming towards the group;

single up – get into single file;

stopping – stopping, or

slowing/easy – slowing due to junction, etc., ahead;

on the left – there is an obstacle on the left, e.g. pedestrian, parked car;

pothole – pothole (and point towards it).

Accidents

In case of an accident, stay calm and, if needed, ring the emergency services on 999. It is a good idea to carry a basic first aid kit and perhaps also one of the commercial foil wraps to put around anyone who has an accident to keep them warm. If someone comes off their bicycle move them and the bike off the road if it is safe to do so. Get someone in the party to warn approaching traffic to slow down, and if necessary ring for an ambulance.

Cycling off-road

All the routes in this book take you along legal rights of way – bridleways, byways open to all traffic and roads used as public paths – it is illegal to cycle along footpaths. Generally the off-road sections of the routes will be easy if the weather and ground are dry. If the weather has been wet and the ground is muddy, it is not a good idea to cycle along bridleways unless you do not mind getting dirty and unless you have a mountain bike which will not get blocked up with mud. In dry weather any bicycle will be able to cover the bridleway sections, but you may need to dismount if the path is very uneven.

Off-road cycling is different to cycling on the road. The average speed is lower, you will use more energy, your riding style will be different and there is a different set of rules to obey – the off-road code:

1 Give way to horse riders and pedestrians, and use a bell or call out to warn someone of your presence.
2 Take your rubbish with you.
3 Do not light fires.
4 Close gates behind you.
5 Do not interfere with wildlife, plants or trees.
6 Use only tracks where you have a right of way, or where the landowner has given you permission to ride.
7 Avoid back wheel skids, which can start erosion gulleys and ruin the bridleway.

Some of the off-road rides take you some miles from shelter and civilisation – take waterproofs, plenty of food and drink and basic tools – especially spare inner tubes and tyre repair equipment. Tell someone where you are going and approximately when you are due back. You are more likely to tumble off your bike riding off-road, so you should consider wearing a helmet and mittens with padded palms.

Local Tourist Information Centres

Alton
7 Cross and Pillory Lane, Alton
Telephone (01420) 88448

Beaulieu
John Montague Building, Beaulieu
Telephone (01590) 612345

Blandford Forum
Marsh and Ham Car Park, West Street, Blandford
Telephone (01258) 454770

Bridport
32 South Street, Bridport
Telephone (01308) 424901

Dorchester
Antelope Walk, Dorchester
Telephone (01305) 267992

Lyme Regis
Church Street, Lyme Regis
Telephone (01297) 442138

Lymington
St Barbe Museum, Lymington
Telephone (01590) 672422

Petersfield
Country Library, The Square, Petersfield
Telephone (01730) 268829

Poole
Poole Quay, Poole
Telephone (01202) 253253

Purbeck
Trinity Church, South Street, Purbeck
(01929) 552740

Petersfield
Country Library, The Square, Petersfield
Telephone (01730) 268829

Ringwood
Furlong Car Park, Ringwood
Telephone (01425) 470896

Ryde
81-3 Union Street, Ryde
Telephone (01983) 562905

Shaftesbury
8 Bell Street, Shaftesbury
(01747) 853514

Sherborne
3 Tilton Court, Digby Road, Sherborne
Telephone (01935) 815341

Weymouth
The Esplanade, Weymouth
Telephone (01305) 785747

Wimborne
29 High Street, Wimborne
Telephone (01202) 886116

Winchester
Guildhall, The Broadway, Winchester
Telephone (01962) 840500

Yarmouth
The Quay, Yarmouth
Telephone (01983) 760015

Local cycle hire

Autovogue
140 High Street, Ryde
Telephone (01983) 812989

Battersby Cycles
2 Hill Street, Ryde
Telephone (01983) 562039

Dorchester Cycles
31 Great Western Road, Dorchester
Telephone (01305) 268787

Peter Hansford
4 London Road, Horndean
Telephone (01705) 592270

Isle Cycle Hire
Wavells Fine Foods, The Square, Yarmouth
Telephone (01983) 760219

New Forest Cycle Hire
Island Shop, Brookley Road, Brockenhurst
Telephone (01590) 624204

Owens Cycles
Lavant Street, Petersfield
Telephone (01730) 260446

Local cycle shops

Autovogue, Battersby Cycles, Dorchester Cycles, Peter Hansford and Owens Cycles.

C.B. Ransomes
86 Victoria Street, Alton
Telephone (01420) 82867

Shepherds Cycles
319 Ashley Road, Parkstone, Poole
Telephone (01202) 742180

Wareham Sports and Cycles
28 South Street, Wareham
Telephone (01929) 552774

P.J. Watts Cycles
3 Station Road, Alresford
Telephone (01962) 733145

Westham Cycles
128 Abbotsbury Road, Weymouth
Telephone (01305) 776977

Route **1**

NEW ALRESFORD TO FOUR MARKS – HAMPSHIRE'S STEAM RAILWAY

Route information

Distance 12km (7.5 miles)

Grade Easy

Terrain Mostly minor roads. The return route from Four Marks to Alresford is almost entirely downhill.

Time to allow 1–3 hours.

Getting there by car Alresford is just north of the A31 Winchester/Farnham road, on the B3047. There is a pay and display car park at the station.

Getting there by train South West Trains run a service from London (Waterloo) via Woking direct to Alton, telephone (0345) 484950 for information. At Alton, change onto the Watercress Line steam train, alight at Medstead & Four Marks station and cycle the route to Alresford, from where you can catch a return steam train to Alton. The Watercress Line rolling stock is equipped with traditional guards vans which can carry your bicycle.

From Alresford to Four Marks on the Mid-Hants Watercress Line, Hampshire's steam railway. Alight at Medstead & Four Marks station and return to Alresford by bicycle, along country lanes.

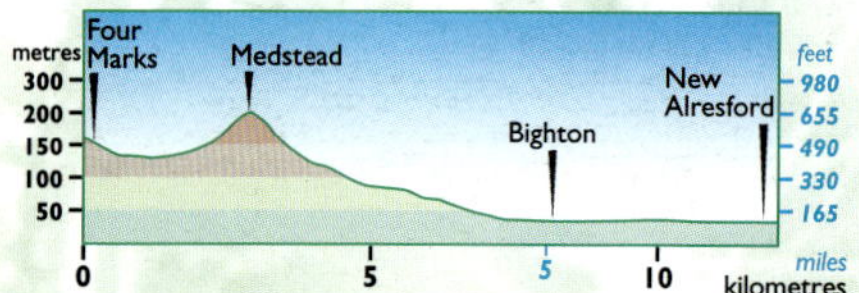

Places of interest along the route

A Watercress Line, between Alresford and Alton

The last normal service steam trains ran in this region in 1967, and in 1977 the newly renovated Watercress Line ran their first train between Alresford and Ropley. Passengers can now travel between Alresford and Alton, through Ropley and Medstead & Four Marks stations, on preserved steam trains. The complete round trip takes around 2 hours, the journey between Alresford and Medstead & Four Marks stations around 25 minutes. Alresford station is the headquarters of the Watercress Line and has a buffet and gift shop. A return ticket allows you to make as many train journeys as you wish in one day – Ropley station, famous for its topiary, is the engineering centre of the railway, where all the engines and coaches are restored. There is also a picnic site and station shop. Medstead & Four Marks, a quiet country station, is the highest station in southern England. From its footbridge you can watch the engines work up the steep hill from Ropley. The Watercress Line links up with the national railway system at Alton, where there is a station shop and information kiosk. Special events and days out are run throughout the year. Alresford station is open daily, all year (except Christmas Day). Charge. Telephone (01962) 734866 for the talking timetable; (01962) 733810 for general information.

B Alresford

Alresford is an attractive, Georgian town with wide tree-lined streets. It is the location of watercress beds, from where the railway took its name. The causeway between New and Old Alresford retains a pond (originally 200 acres/ 81ha, now 30 acres/12ha), built by Bishop Godfrey, circa 1200 AD, in order to dam the River Arle and provide additional water for the Itchen Navigation. The pond is now home to wildfowl and otters.

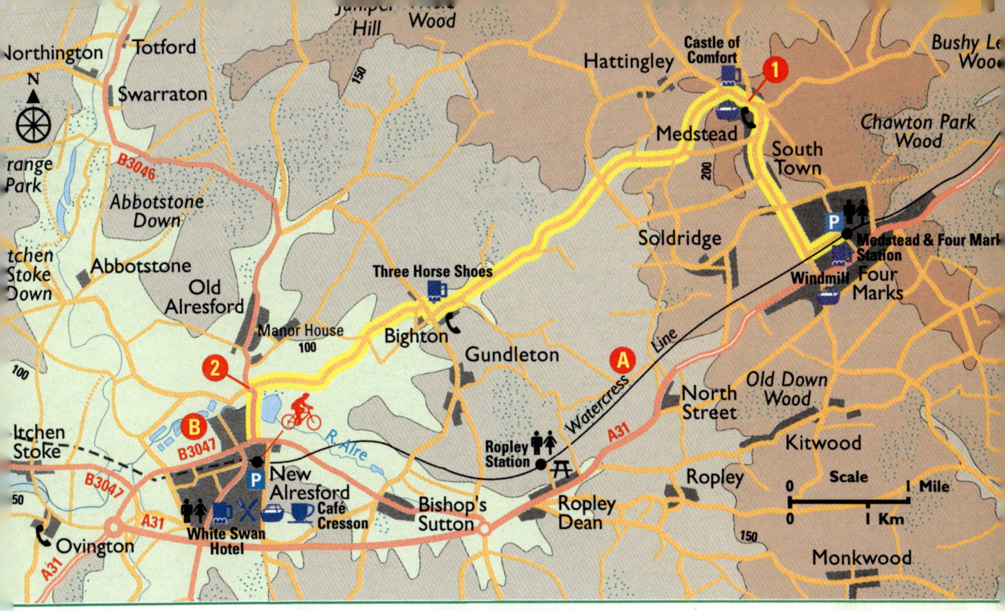

Hill
Wood
Northington
Totford
Swarraton
Hattingley
Castle of Comfort
Bushy Lea Wood
Medstead
South Town
Chawton Park Wood
Grange Park
B3046
Abbotstone Down
Soldridge
Medstead & Four Marks Station
Itchen Stoke Down
Abbotstone
Old Alresford
Three Horse Shoes
Windmill
Four Marks
Manor House
Bighton
Gundleton
Watercress Line
Old Down Wood
North Street
Itchen Stoke
B3047
R. Alre
Ropley Station
A31
Kitwood
New Alresford
Ropley
Scale
Mile
Km
Café Cresson
Bishop's Sutton
Ropley Dean
White Swan Hotel
Ovington
Monkwood

Route description 

The approach to Alresford station is well signposted. Board a train at the station. Alight at Medstead & Four Marks station and TL outside the station. At TJ TR (no SP). Four Marks itself is on your right. Continue to Medstead.

1 In Medstead TL at TJ (High Street). TL SP Bighton and Alresford (9.5km/6 miles). Continue through Bighton to TJ with B3046.

2 At TJ TL over causeway and return to Alresford.

12km (7.5 miles)

Food and drink 

There is a small shopping centre in Four Marks, opposite the Windmill pub. Village shops can also be found in Medstead (The Handy Stores), and in Alresford (Country News, Balfour News and the Co-op). Alresford has several places to eat including the Café Cresson, Horse and Groom and the Bell pubs.

Watercress Line
Buffet at Alresford station. All trains usually have a licensed buffet.

Windmill, Four Marks
Large, comfortable pub serving teas and coffees, and a large selection of bar meals and snacks.

Castle of Comfort, Medstead
Teas, coffees and bar snacks available at lunchtimes only.

Three Horse Shoes, Bighton
Small and pleasant traditional pub serving bar snacks at lunchtimes (except Mondays).

White Swan Hotel, Alresford
The hotel serves everything from a cup of tea to a full meal, all day. Popular with local cyclists.

Route **2**

SHAFTESBURY – MELBURY DOWN AND ZIG ZAG HILL

Route information

Distance 15km (9.5 miles)

Grade Easy (one long climb)

Terrain Hilly but well-tarmacked roads. Suitable for most types of bicycle, but low gears will be needed for the first half of the ride.

Time to allow 1–3 hours.

Getting there by car Shaftesbury is off the A30 Salisbury to Yeovil road. There is limited town centre parking.

Getting there by train Gillingham (Dorset) is the nearest station, approximately 6.5km (4 miles) northwest from Shaftesbury, along the B3081.

From the hilltop town of Shaftesbury, famous for Gold Hill and splendid views over Melbury Down and Cranborne Chase, this route drops down from Shaftesbury and then climbs, steeply at first, up Compton Down – offering magnificent views of Fontmell Down and Melbury Hill and their ancient earthworks, dykes, mounds and tumuli. The climb, whilst long, is not difficult if tackled at a steady pace in a low gear, and is well worth the effort. The route continues along a ridge, with Melbury Wood to the left and Ashmore Down to the right, and extensive views of Dorset and Cranborne Chase. Then, a long steady descent begins, culminating in the zig zags of Zig Zag Hill and the return, via Cann Common, to Shaftesbury.

Places of interest along the route

A Shaftesbury Town Museum, Gold Hill, Shaftesbury

Shaftesbury, an ancient Saxon hilltop town, contains more history in one square mile than any other settlement in Dorset. The museum is housed in a small cottage at the top of Gold Hill, Shaftesbury's most famous landmark. Each room in the cottage contains many objects relating to the town's fascinating history and locality. The intriguing exhibits include a collection of Anglo-Saxon coins, a display of Dorset buttons and a wooden fire engine dating from 1744. Cottage garden alongside museum. Open from Easter to the end of September, daily 1100–1700. Charge. Telephone (01747) 852157 or 854548 for further information.

B Shaftesbury Abbey and Museum, Park Walk, Shaftesbury

Shaftesbury Abbey, a Benedictine house for women, was founded circa 888 AD by King Alfred the Great for his daughter Aethelgifu, the first abbess. The abbey acted as a catalyst for the prosperity of the town and surrounding area for over 700 years, and patronage and pilgrimage made the abbey rich and famous during Medieval times. The religious life of the abbey ended on the Dissolution of the monasteries by Henry VIII in 1539 and the buildings fell into disrepair. Many of the local houses are thought to be built partly of stone from the abbey ruins. The abbey remains have been excavated over the past 150 years and are on view (self-guided tour describes the ruins). The museum contains a collection of carved stonework and medieval floor tiles. In the garden is a reconstructed Anglo Saxon herb bed. Open from Easter to October, daily 1000–1700.Charge. Telephone (01747) 852910 for information.

C Melbury Down

This chalk downland is at the northern edge of Cranborne Chase, once the royal hunting grounds of King John. Now designated an area of outstanding natural beauty and owned by the National Trust.

D Win Green

The highest point of Cranborne Chase at 273m (896 feet), and strictly in Wiltshire. Its distinctive clump of trees shields a bowl barrow. Views, on clear days, to the Isle of Wight and the Quantocks. Owned by the National Trust.

E Zig Zag Hill

On your return to Shaftesbury, Zig Zag Hill is well known by local cyclists who like to do strange things such as ride up it to celebrate 70th birthdays!

Food and drink

Shaftesbury has numerous pubs and cafés.

Compton Abbas Airfield Restaurant, near Shaftesbury

En route, about a third of the way into the ride. Enjoy marvellous views and anything from breakfast and morning coffee to afternoon tea and evening bar snacks. Open daily 0900–sunset.

Gold Hill, Shaftesbury

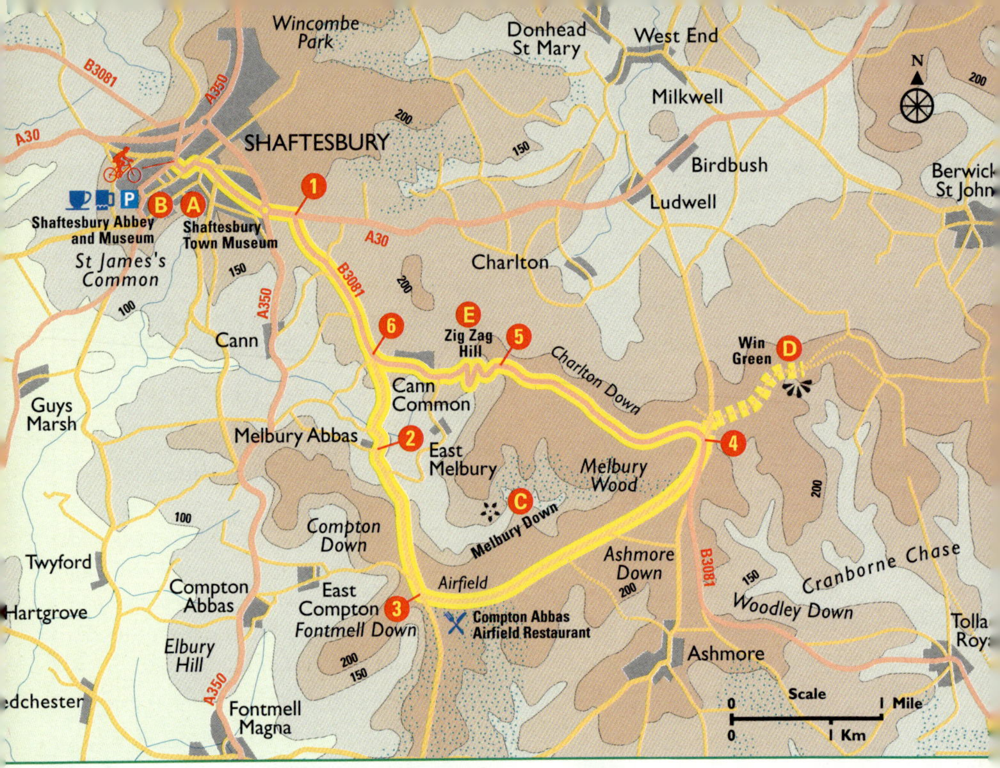

Route description 

Leave Shaftesbury along the A30 (Salisbury road). SO at the roundabout with A350 (Blandford road).

1 TR onto the B3081, Higher Blandford Road.

2 Arrive at Melbury Abbas, and begin the climb of Compton Down, along the side of Melbury Hill (known locally as Spreadeagle Hill).

3 TL at the top of the hill passing Compton Abbas Airfield on the left. ***5km (3 miles)***

4 Bear left onto B3081. To visit Win Green, take the bridleway on the right, SP Win Green. ***8km (5 miles)***

5 Descend Zig Zag Hill, with care, into Cann Common.

6 TR and follow road back to A30 and Shaftesbury. ***15km (9.5 miles)***

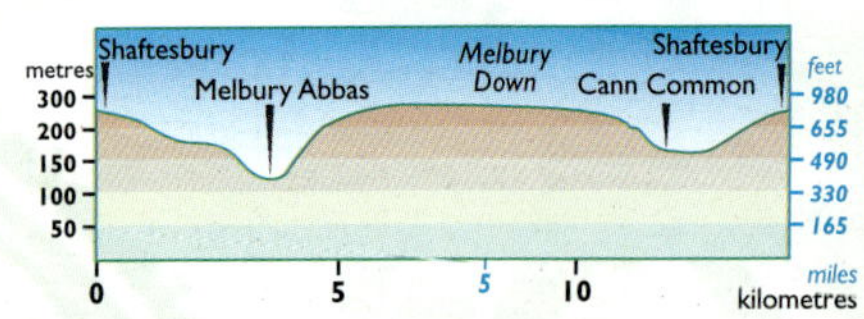

Route 3

DORCHESTER AND MAIDEN CASTLE

Route information

Distance 16.5km (10.5 miles)

Grade Easy

Terrain Mostly unclassified flat minor roads, some town streets and two sections of bridleway.

Time to allow 1–3 hours.

Getting there by car Dorchester is on the A35 Folkestone to Honiton road. Car parking is available in the market area between the two railway stations.

Getting there by train Dorchester is on the Waterloo to Weymouth main line and has a frequent service. It is also on a line that intersects with Yeovil Junction. Telephone (0345) 484950 for information.

Out from Dorchester, passing the ancient earthworks of the Maumbury Rings, towards Maiden Castle. The bridleway up to Maiden Castle is quite strenuous, but after this the narrow unclassified lanes are all flat and make for easy cycling. Pass through the Came estate heading for Stinsford on the east of Dorchester, before returning towards the town centre via road or bridleway.

Places of interest along the route

A Dorchester

Dorchester is the County Town of Dorset and has many old streets and buildings. It is well known as the writer Thomas Hardy's Casterbridge. High West Street runs through the centre of town to the Top o' Town, where the statue of Thomas Hardy can be seen. Dorset's other poet, William Barnes, can be found halfway up High West Street. The **Keep Military Museum**, at Top o' Town, displays 300 years of military history in an interesting listed building. There are medals, weapons and uniforms to see, together with touch pad displays and videos. Great views from the battlements. Open all year, Monday–Friday 0930–1700, Saturday 0930–1300 and 1400–1700. Charge. Telephone (01305) 264066. **Dorset County Museum** is on High West Street. This award-winning museum features local geology, archaeology, natural and local history, including the story of Maiden Castle, a recreation of Thomas Hardy's study and an interactive Writers Gallery. Open all year, Monday–Saturday 1000–1700; in addition, July and August, Sunday 1000–1700. Charge. Telephone (01305) 262735. The **Tutankhamun Exhibition**, in High West Street, recreates Tutankhamun's tomb and treasure through sight, sound and smell. Open all year, daily 0930–1730. Charge. Telephone (01305) 269571. The **Teddy Bear House**, in Antelope Walk, is where you can meet Edward Bear and his family of human-sized bears, as they relax at home or busy themselves in the Old Dorset Teddy Bear factory. Open May to August, daily 0930–1730, September to April hours vary – please check opening times. Charge. Telephone (01305) 263200. Dorset also has a Dinosaur Museum and the Old Crown Court and Cells. Telephone the Tourist Information Centre on (01305) 267992 for information.

B Maiden Castle, near Dorchester

An extensive and impressive Iron Age earthwork settlement, dominating the skyline to the southwest of Dorchester. The bridleway passes to the west and another defined path leads up to the original western entrance. Time has softened the outline of this 2000 year old fortified township but the difficulty of mounting an assault may still be judged by any cyclist tackling the approach – unless you retrace your route to the car park, the only way back to the bridleway is to cross the outer fortifications. Construction of the castle was started in 400 BC and at its peak 5000 people lived within its ramparts in wooden huts. The castle was invaded and destroyed by the Romans in 43 AD, who later built the new town of Dorchester (Durnovaria) in around 70 AD. Access at all reasonable times. Admission free. Telephone English Heritage on 0171 973 3434 for further information.

C Kingston Maurward Gardens and Animal Park, near Dorchester

Fine gardens and lawns within parkland, lake, demonstration gardens, the National Collection of Penstemons and Salvias, animal park, visitor centre, nature trail and restaurant. The gardens are maintained in conjunction with the Dorset Agricultural College in Kingston Maurward House, and residential and vocational courses on subjects ranging from horticulture to woodland management are available. Open Easter to October, daily 1000–1730. Charge. Telephone (01305) 264738.

Food and drink

There are many cafés, restaurants, pubs and hotels of all standards in Dorchester but for basic fare the A35 Café at Top o' Town in the car park, known by all local club cyclists, should be visited.

Old Coach House Restaurant, Kingston Maurward

Morning coffee, lunches and cream teas.

Route description

Leave the station car park past Maumbury Rings. SO at traffic lights and over the railway bridge. Be careful along this short stretch of main road as there is a right hand turn coming up.

1 TR SP Maiden Castle, into Maiden Castle Road. There is a cycleway down the left of this road, which is helpful in cutting through the traffic calming restrictions. Cross the bridge over the bypass and the lane becomes more rural. Excellent views of Maiden Castle now as you approach.

2 Take bridleway to the right of car park at the foot of Maiden Castle. Note that the white gravel track that winds up from the car park is not the bridleway but leads to the entrance to the earthwork. If you take this to see the western entrance, you will need to retrace your route to the car park.

3 TL after gate onto tarmac road. No SP. Very narrow road with grass growing down the middle in places. ***3.5km (2 miles)***

4 TL, SP Winterborne Monkton village.

5 Staggered TL and then TR at junction (with right turning lane in centre to make this easier). Cross main road with care. SP Winterborne Herringston. ***5km (3 miles)***

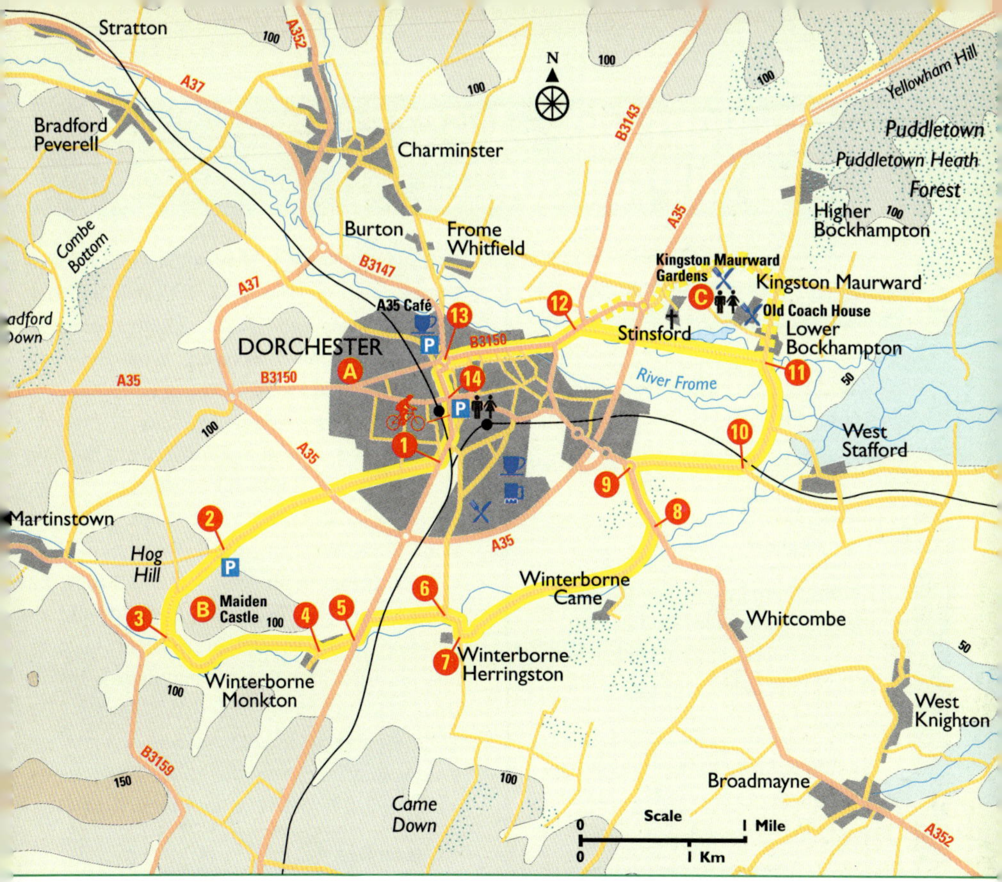

6 TR, no SP. Big country house on the right.

5.5km (3.5 miles)

7 TL, no SP.

8 TL at TJ onto main road for a short stretch. Take care on the first wooded bend.

9 TR at roundabout, SP West Stafford. Pick up the cyclepath on the left hand side of the road.

10km (6 miles)

10 TL over railway bridge, SP Stinsford and Bockhampton.

11 To visit Kingston Maurward, SO, then TL at XR and TL SP Stinsford Church. To return to route, retrace to bridleway (adds 5km/3 miles) or negotiate busy roundabout to return directly to Dorchester (adds 1.5km/1 mile). If not visiting Kingston Maurward, TL onto bridleway just before river, SP Dorchester.

12 At TJ, TL onto road, cross bridge and continue up High Street. Note wording carved into stone of building half way up High Street Hyde Park Corner 120 miles. Pass William Barnes statue and the Dorchester Museum.

14km (8.5 miles)

13 TL at Top o' Town roundabout and follow road round to traffic lights.

14 SO at traffic lights then TL into market area car park.

16.5km (10.5 miles)

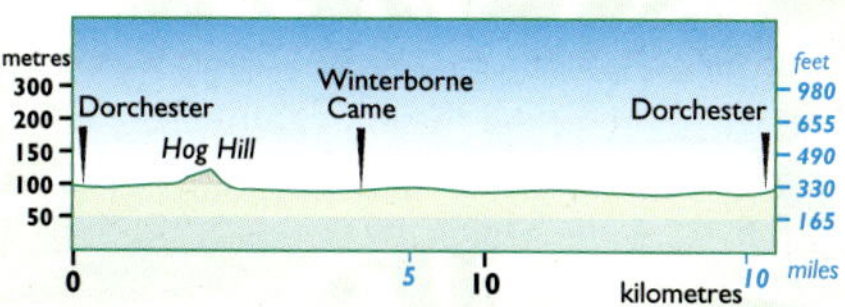

Route 4

BRIDPORT LOOP – WEST BAY AND SHIPTON GORGE

Route information

Distance 18km (11 miles)

Grade Easy

Terrain Coastal scenery and narrow country lanes.

Time to allow 1–3 hours.

Getting there by car Bridport is on the A35 Folkestone–Honiton road. There is a long stay car park in East Street, with toilets close by in the park.

Getting there by train There are no convenient rail links to the start of this route.

From the market town of Bridport to the harbour mouth at West Bay. Then along the coast to Burton Beach before heading inland towards the rugged scenery of Shipton Hill and Shipton Gorge. The route heads back into Bridport through the lovely Dorset villages of Uploders and Loders.

Places of interest along the route

A Bridport

The market town of Bridport became famous in the 13th century for its net and rope-making industries. A market is held on Wednesday and Saturday in South and West Streets. In South Street look for the pleasant and unusually named Buckey Doo Square, situated behind the Town Hall. **Palmers Brewery**, West Bay Road, has been established in the town since 1794 and its beer is available in many of the town pubs. Guided tours of the brewery are conducted Easter to September, Wednesday and Thursday 1100–1315. Charge. Book at Palmers Wine Store, West Bay Road. Telephone (01308) 427500. **Bridport Museum**, South Street, has displays on the history of Bridport and the museum itself (housed in a Tudor building), fine art, rural life, costume and natural history. Open April to October, Monday–Saturday 1000–1700, Sunday 1400–1700; November to March, Wednesday and Saturday 1000–1700, Sunday 1400–1700. Charge. Telephone (01308) 422116.

B West Bay

West Bay has a unique harbour, at the mouth of the River Brit, which defines the westernmost end of Chesil Beach. It is a busy fishing village with all the atmosphere and entertainment you would expect from the harbour kiosks and fishing boats. The **Harbour Museum** is in a converted salt house overlooking the harbour. The museum tells the story of Bridport's famous net and rope-making industry and the history of Bridport Harbour. Open April to October, daily 1000–1800. Charge. Telephone (01308) 420997.

C Burton Beach

The beach associated with Burton Bradstock is an excellent place for a picnic with lovely views around Lyme Bay and of Chesil Beach. Cliff and riverside walks.

Burton Bradstock

D Old Farming Collection, Bredy Farm

A collection of old farm and estate equipment and an ancient sawmill, situated on a working stock and arable farm. Open Spring Bank Holiday to September, daily 1030–1730. Charge. Telephone (01308) 897229.

E Loders

Visit the 12th-century Church of St Mary Magdalen – charming inside and out. Early 13th-century font and 15th-century painted glass and sculpture.

Route description

TL leaving the car park in East Street, towards the town centre. At the traffic lights TL into South Street, SP West Bay. Continue past Palmers Brewery to Crown Roundabout.

1 Take the third exit off the roundabout, SP West Bay. The road can be busy at times, so as an alternative use the pedestrian subway to the right of the roundabout.

2 Arrive West Bay. At TJ, TL SP Burton Bradstock. Or, TR to explore West Bay and its harbour.

3 TR at TJ, SP Weymouth. Ride through Burton Bradstock. After crossing the bridge, take LHF ignoring the road to the right.

4 To visit Burton Beach TR, SP Hive Beach Café. To continue route TL, SP Litton Cheney. ***6km (3.5 miles)***

5 TL SP Shipton Gorge, passing Bredy Farm on the left. Continue to top of hill and look ahead for the lovely views of Shipton Gorge and the unusually shaped Shipton Hill.

6 SO at XR SP Loders & Bridport. (The village of Shipton Gorge is to the left.)

10km (6 miles)

7 TR no SP.

8 Pass under the A35 and continue to Uploders.

9 TL by The Crown, SP Bridport, and follow the lane down to the picturesque village of Loders.

10 TL SP Bridport. ***15km (9.5 miles)***

11 At A3066, TL to Bridport.

12 TR SP Police Station (St Andrews Road), and follow through to Barrack Street. Cross East Street to return to car park and the end of the route. ***18km (11 miles)***

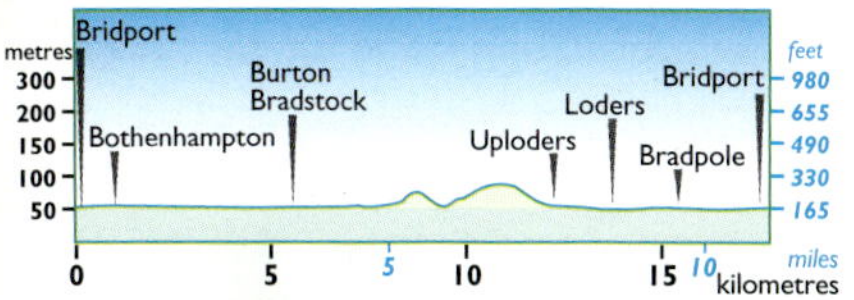

Food and drink 

Bridport has many pubs and cafés, some serving local seafood. There are several pubs and a village shop in Burton Bradstock.

Riverside Café, West Bay
Grills and snacks on the banks of the River Brit.

Hive Beach Café, Burton Beach
Teas and ice creams on the beach.

The Anchor, Burton Bradstock
Local ales, teas and coffees. Bar snacks at lunchtime, à la carte meals in the evening.

The Crown, Uploders
Cyclist friendly pub – if you are travelling in a group, please let them know in advance. Local ales and bar meals.

West Bay

Route 5

MOTTISFONT, HOUGHTON AND STOCKBRIDGE

Route information

Distance 21.5km (13.5 miles)

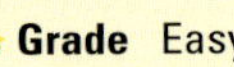

Grade Easy

Terrain Unclassified roads and all-weather gravel cycle tracks (except for a short distance on the A3057 at the start of the ride, and where the A30 becomes Stockbridge Main Street). Mountain bikes are not essential.

Time to allow 2–3 hours if with young children.

Getting there by car The start of the route, Stonymarsh car park, is about 6.5km (4 miles) north of Romsey on the west side of the A3057 (Romsey to Stockbridge road), 0.5km (0.3 miles) north of the Mottisfont turn off.

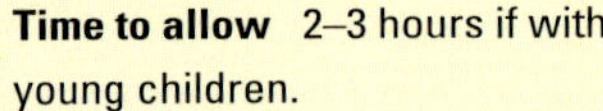

Getting there by train The nearest railway station is at Romsey 6.5km (4 miles) from the start of the route. Telephone (0345) 484950 for information on trains.

A gentle ride using byroads between Mottisfont and Stockbridge, returning along a cycle track popular with families and young children.

Places of interest along the route

A Mottisfont Abbey, Mottisfont

Mottisfont Abbey, located on Mottisfont Estate, was originally a priory, founded in 1201. At the Dissolution, the priory was converted into a house. When the estate was sold in 1934, it was bought by a descendent of the original founder. The estate was gifted to the National Trust in 1957. The house contains a room decorated by Rex Whistler and the Derek Hill Collection of late 19th and early 20th-century pictures. The grounds contain a rose garden (the National Collection of old-fashioned shrub roses), mill stream, spring (or font – from where Mottisfont takes its name), pollarded lime walk and river walks where waterfowl, kingfishers and herons may be seen. Restaurant. Open March to October, Saturday–Wednesday 1200–1800 (or dusk if earlier); Whistler Room open 1300–1700; Derek Hill Collection open Sunday–Tuesday 1300–1700. The best time to see the rose garden is June and July when it is open daily 1200–2030. Charge. Telephone (01794) 340757.

B Houghton Lodge Gardens, North Houghton

Eighteenth-century cottage, hydroponicum (plants growing entirely without soil), and beautiful gardens leading down to the River Test, where you may see swans gliding over the water. Often used for film locations. Open March to September, weekends and Bank Holidays 1000–1700, Monday–Tuesday and

Thursday–Friday 1400–1700; closed Wednesday. Charge. Telephone (01264) 810177.

C Stockbridge

There has been a settlement at Stockbridge for many hundreds of years. Buildings in the High Street are constructed on an old causeway of chalk and bundles of withies laid over the marshy valley of the River Test. The Romans settled in this area and Stockbridge lies at the junction of the east-west Roman road between Winchester, Old Sarum and Salisbury, and the north-south Roman road from Newbury to Southampton. The distinctive Town Hall was built in 1790 and paid for by John Barham MP as an election bribe. The town has been the site of regular markets since the 12th century and, in more recent centuries, horse racing meetings (race horse training continued near Stockbridge into the 20th century). Edward, Prince of Wales, stayed in Stockbridge for the races, while Lillie Langtry stayed across the river. The Drovers Cottage on the Houghton Road was formerly an inn. It was used by Welsh drovers driving their sheep to Southampton and an inscription in Welsh on the cottage walls is translated as seasoned hay, tasty pasture, good food and a comfortable bed. Arms of the River Test run under the main street and fish may be easily observed.

Food and drink

There are tearooms at Mottisfont and Stockbridge, and several pubs and restaurants in Stockbridge.

The Boot, Houghton
Real ale and bar snacks.

John O' Gaunt, Horsebridge
Ale and bar snacks.

Houghton Lodge Gardens

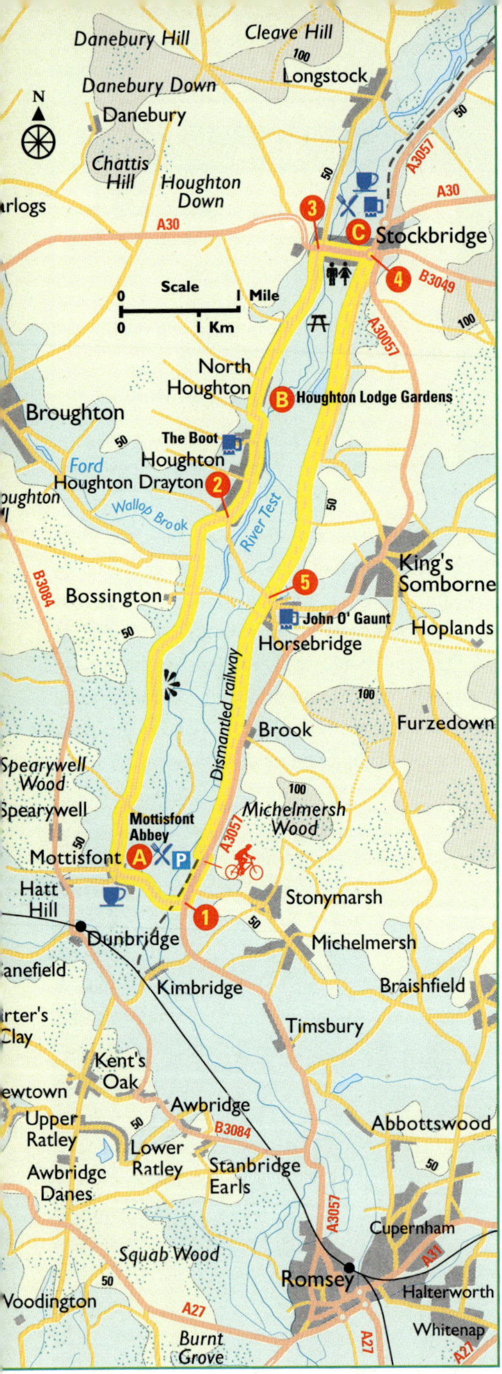

Route description

From the Stonymarsh car park TR and continue south for 0.5km (0.3 miles).

1 TR, SP Mottisfont and Mottisfont Abbey. The road bears right through Mottisfont village. Continue to Houghton. In spring, bluebell woods on left after 3km (2 miles). Views over the Test valley to the right.

2 TL, SP Stockbridge and Houghton Lodge Gardens, passing Houghton Lodge Gardens on the right. ***7km (4.5 miles)***

3 At XR TR onto A30 (with care) and continue over the main channel of the Test into Stockbridge. ***12km (7.5 miles)***

4 At the eastern end of Stockbridge either take the last exit from the roundabout at Trafalgar Way or (especially if with children) TR before the roundabout at New Street and use the service road to Trafalgar Way. Join the cycle track at the end of Trafalgar Way and continue to Horsebridge. This part of the cycle track is popular with birdwatchers.

5 At Horsebridge the cycle track crosses the road. Continue on cycle track and return to car park. ***21.5km (13.5 miles)***

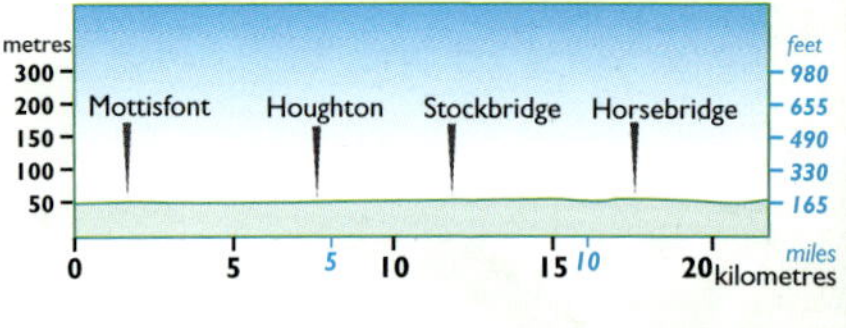

Route 6

POOLE LOOP – HOLES BAY, UPTON AND WIMBORNE

Route information

Distance 23.5km (14.5 miles)

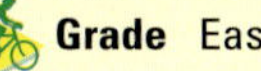

Grade Easy

Terrain Flat cycleways and a few quiet roads. The Roman road bridleway climbs steadily.

Time to allow 2–3 hours.

Getting there by car From Ringwood and the east Poole can be reached via the M3, M27 and A348. From Dorchester and the west use the A35. From the M4 in the north, Poole is now SP all the way from Chippenham. To reach the start of the route, follow SP to Baiter and use either of the two car parks.

Getting there by train Poole is on the main Waterloo to Weymouth line and there is a frequent service. There is a regular through train service from the Midlands. Telephone (0345) 484950 for information.

Poole has an extensive and increasingly inter-linked network of cycleways and cycle parking racks. This route takes you from Baiter, in Poole, on the cycleway leading west along Poole Quay, then onto the main cycleway out of Poole, running alongside Holes Bay up to Upton Country Park. This section of the route will be even more pleasant if you time your ride when the tide is high. You then head north along the track of a Roman road to Merley, turning along a quiet country lane and a disused road before returning to Poole by way of the Castleman Trailway (on the site of an old railway line) and the other side of Poole's main cycleway.

Places of interest along the route

A Poole

Baiter (Bay Tor), at the start of the ride, is largely reclaimed land. It was the site of the old Poole gallows, and the burial ground for victims of the Black Death, but is now a pleasant green park. The economy of Poole is a healthy balance of tourism and commerce and Poole Quay bustles with life at all times of the year. **Poole Pottery** has been established on Poole Quay since 1873. On site is a museum, factory shop, craft village and café. Visitors can tour the factory and see the pottery being created, watch craftsmen at work and have a go at making or decorating pottery themselves. Museum factory tour open throughout the year 1000–1600 (except weekends in winter). Various parts of the site do open and close at different times during the year, so please telephone before visiting. Charge. Telephone (01202) 666200. The **Aquarium Complex**, Poole Quay, concentrates on the wonders of the natural world with aquarium, serpentarium, dinosaurs, crocodiles, insects and other creepy crawlies, and a scenic model railway. Coffee shop. Open daily throughout the year, March to June 1000–1730, July and August 0900–2100, September and October 1000–1730, November to February 1000–1700. Note that opening periods may vary, please telephone to confirm. Telephone (01202) 686712. The **Waterfront**

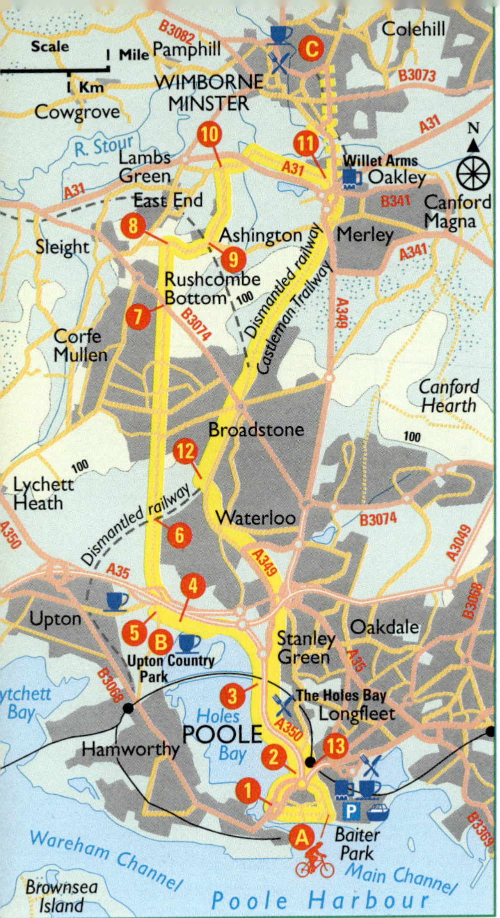

Museum, Poole Quay, tells of Poole's seafaring past, from the Roman occupation, to smugglers and the first scout camp in 1907. Victorian tea-room and craft shop. Open daily, Easter to June 1000–1700; July and August 1000–1900; September and October 1000–1700; November to March please telephone for details. Charge. Telephone (01202) 683138. En route, in West Quay Road is the headquarters and **Museum of the RNLI**. Open all year, except weekends and public holidays, 0930–1630. Admission free. Telephone (01202) 663000 for information.

B Upton Country Park, Upton

Country estate of over 40.5ha (100 acres) run by the Borough of Poole. Specimen trees and shrubs, rose garden and herbaceous borders surround the early 19th-century Upton House. Landscaped gardens lead to farmland, wood-land and saltmarsh, which all support a variety of wildlife. Countryside Heritage Centre introduces visitors to the park and contains displays, crafts, exhibitions and refreshments. Open daily throughout the year, 0900–dusk. Admission free. Telephone (01202) 633514.

C Wimborne Minster

Wimborne Minster is a charming market town containing many beautiful and historic buildings. The Minster itself, the Church of St Cuthburga, was founded in 705 AD and dominates the town's skyline. It contains fine Norman architecture, and a famous astronomical clock, the Quarterjack, a life-sized soldier who strikes the quarter hours on bells. Open daily throughout the year, 0930–1730. The **Model Town and Gardens** comprise one-tenth size models of the town as it was in the early 1950s, set in beautiful landscaped gardens. Exhibition Centre displays miniature working railway and an Old English Fair. Open daily, March to September 1000–1700. Charge. Refreshments, gift shop and plant sales. Telephone (01202) 881924. **Walford Mill Craft Centre** is in a converted water mill on the northern outskirts of Wimborne Minster. Exhibition gallery, craft shop and two workshops. Riverside restaurant. Open daily throughout the year (except Mondays January to March), 1000–1700. Admission free. Telephone (01202) 841400. The **Priest's House Museum** is housed in one of Wimborne's oldest buildings and has a beautiful walled garden. A series of period rooms takes the visitor back through the centuries with a Victorian ironmongers, stationers and kitchen, 18th-century parlour, 17th-century hall and a Childhood Gallery, where children of all ages can play with the toys. Tearoom and gift shop. Open April to October, Monday–Saturday 1030–1700; June to September, also Sundays and Bank Holidays 1400–1700. Telephone (01202) 882533.

Food and drink

Poole and Poole Quay have pubs, restaurants and cafés to suit all requirements, from exclusive restaurants to seafood and burger kiosks. Refreshments also available at Upton Country Park and in Wimborne Minster.

Willett Arms, Merley
Bar snacks and local ales.

The Holes Bay
Travelodge and Restaurant.

Route description

From Baiter join the cycleway by the waterfront and travel west to join Poole Quay. Walk along the short stretch of quay to the Old Customs House and then remount on the road to the bridge.

1 Cross road with care and TR into West Quay Road. Pass RNLI HQ and Museum on your right.

2 At north end of West Quay Road, at Hunger Hill intersection, join pavement/cycleway on left which runs alongside the Holes Bay road.

3 Before reaching the railway, TR to follow the path up and over with views of Pergins Island to your left.

4 Tarmac cycleway becomes track through woods, winds through gate (normally open during the day) SP Broadstone, and follows a wide drovers road alongside Upton Country Park to the main entrance. TL to visit Country Park and retrace to main entrance to rejoin route. ***5.5km (3.5 miles)***

5 Leave Country Park SP Broadstone, cross slip road and then TL SP Castleman Cyclepath. Care needed here at three intersections with road system.

6 Join Roman road SP Broadstone. SO under old railway bridge. Roman road joins tarmac road section, crosses Gladelands Way, becomes short section of bridleway/footpath, crosses Springdale Road and continues (hidden by the bus shelter at Lancaster Drive).

7 Cross Higher Merley (staggered junction) to continue on Roman road bridlepath.
10km (6 miles)

8 TR into Merley Park Road just after Heatherwood Garden Centre.

9 TL into Ashington Lane.

10 TR at TJ, no SP, then through gate SP BR114 Wimborne. ***12km (7.5 miles)***

11 To visit Wimborne TL at main road, over old bridge and keep left all the way into town centre. Otherwise cross main road at cycleway intersection, TR and cross side road to Willett Arms. TL to join Castleman Trailway SP Broadstone.

12 After Broadstone underpass, watch for Trailway crossing old railway bridge – leave Trailway by slip path to right just before bridge. Cycle down and under this bridge to road. No SP. Cross road by controlled intersection and join cycleway on opposite side. Follow cycleway to Poole. ***18km (11 miles)***

13 Pass under the Towngate Bridge and carefully follow cycleway across road and alongside the bridge to the front of the office buildings into North Street (buses and cycles only), cross roundabout and slip through into Green Road and Baiter.
23.5km (14.5 miles)

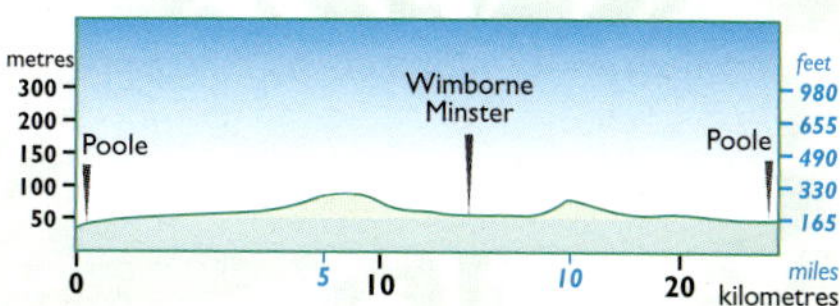

Route 7

WINCHESTER AND THE ITCHEN VALLEY

Route information

Distance 33km (20.5 miles)

Grade Easy

Terrain Mostly quiet byroads with no major hills. The route climbs to its highest point after Itchen Abbas and there is another short climb after Easton. The alternative off-road track before Alresford is also quite easy.

Time to allow 2–2½ hours easy riding, but worth allowing yourself more time.

Getting there by car Winchester is easily accessible from the M3, A34, A31 and A303. There is a long stay car park in Worthy Lane, a few minutes from the railway station.

Getting there by train There is a good train service to Winchester from London Waterloo, Southampton and Poole and there are also direct services from Scotland, the north-east, the northwest and the Midlands. Telephone (0345) 484950 for information.

From Winchester, the route travels through the Itchen Valley to Alresford, before returning to Winchester on the south side of the River Itchen (possibly Charles Kingsley's inspiration for The Water Babies*).*

Places of interest along the route

A Winchester

Winchester has been occupied since 450 BC and was the Saxon capital of England. With so much to see, you could take days to fully explore the city. **Winchester Cathedral**, The Close, was begun in 1079 and encompasses the Triforium Gallery (sculpture, woodwork and metalwork from 1100 years of the cathedral's history), the picturesque close itself, and visitor centre (shop and restaurant). Open daily all year, 0715–1830 (restricted access during services). Free admission, but suggested donation. Telephone (01962) 853137. The **Great Hall**, Castle Avenue, is the only surviving part of Winchester Castle and contains the legendary Arthurian Round Table and a recreated medieval garden. Open all year, daily 1000–1700; weekends in winter 1000–1600. Free admission. Telephone (01962) 846476 for information. There are many other visitor attractions in Winchester, including the **Military Museums**, **Jane Austen's House**, the **medieval residences of the Bishops of Winchester** and the 18th-century **City Mill**. The Tourist Information Centre will be able to give full details.

B New Alresford

Alresford was founded in the 12th century by Bishop de Lucy, and was mentioned in the Domesday Book. The Georgian architecture and fine streets seen today were constructed after great fires in the 17th century. The causeway between New and Old Alresford retains a pond (originally 200 acres/81ha, now 30 acres/

12ha), built by Bishop Godfrey, circa 1200 AD, in order to dam the River Arle and provide additional water for the Itchen Navigation. The pond is now home to wildfowl and otters.

C Itchen Valley

The real attraction of this ride must be the combination of natural and man-made beauty of the Itchen Valley – Ovington is a good place from which to admire the River Itchen. Itchen Abbas, on the north side of the river, is where Charles Kingsley is said to have written *The Water Babies*. Water from the Itchen was used to create the lake at **Avington Park** (a place often visited by Charles II and Nell Gwynne), the setting for Avington House, a Georgian mansion with Tudor origins and uniquely painted and decorated rooms. Tearoom. Open May to September, Sundays and Bank Holidays 1430–1730. Charge. Telephone (01962) 779260. **Avington Church** is an unspoilt Georgian church which still retains its original box pews.

City Mill, Winchester

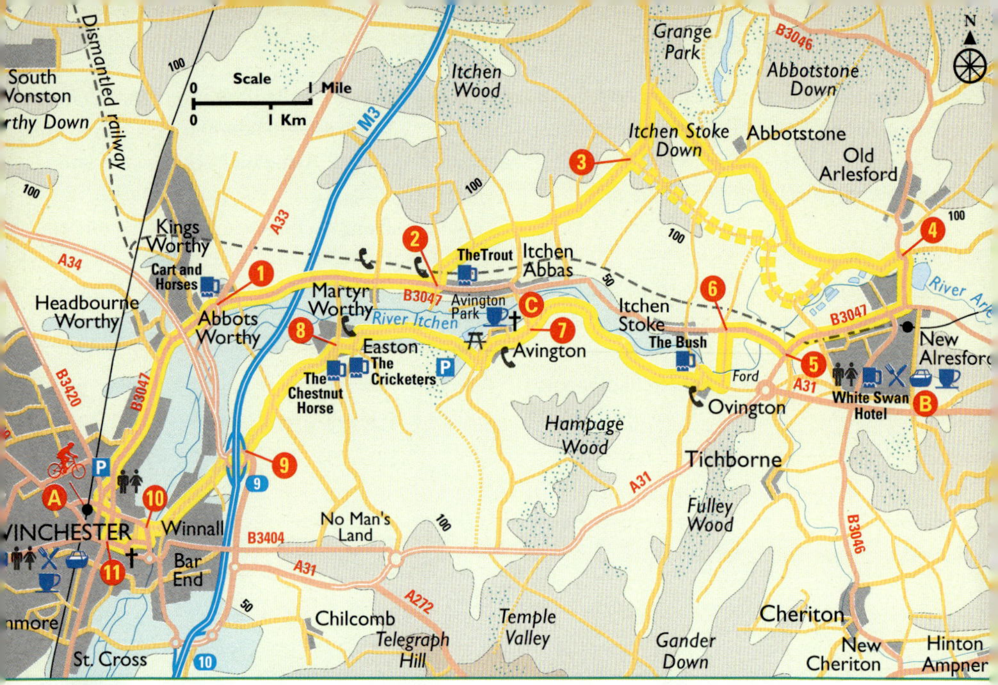

South Wonston
Worthy Down
Dismantled railway
Scale
0 1 Mile
0 1 Km
Itchen Wood
M3
Grange Park
B3046
Abbotstone Down
Itchen Stoke Down
Abbotstone
Old Arlesford
Kings Worthy
A34
A33
Cart and Horses
The Trout
Itchen Abbas
Headbourne Worthy
Abbots Worthy
Martyr Worthy
B3047
Avington Park
River Itchen
Easton
Avington
Itchen Stoke
The Bush
River Arle
New Alresford
The Chestnut Horse
The Cricketers
Ford
A31
Ovington
White Swan Hotel
B3420
B3047
Hampage Wood
Tichborne
Fulley Wood
WINCHESTER
Winnall
No Man's Land
B3404
Bar End
B3046
A31
A272
Chilcomb
Telegraph Hill
Temple Valley
Gander Down
Cheriton
New Cheriton
Hinton Ampner
St. Cross

Route description

From Winchester Station descend to the XR and TL, SP Basingstoke/Newbury/Andover. Then TR into Worthy Lane, SP Basingstoke. From the long stay car park by Worthy Lane, take the exit into Worthy Lane and TL.

1 SO (with care) at staggered XR with A33, SP Alresford.

2 Arrive Itchen Abbas. TL by Village Hall, SP School/Veterinary Control. The Trout pub is 100m around the corner. ***7km (4.5 miles)***

3 For off-road section, TR (take third exit which is almost SO). After crossing stream TR and continue to TJ where TR to rejoin route.

Otherwise, SO to continue route. Then take second right, no SP, and descend to deserted village of Abbotstone. (11km/7 miles). Follow SP to Alresford.

4 Arrive at TJ (16km/10 miles) and TR (no SP) over causeway to Alresford. Then at TJ, SP Winchester, TR.

5 TR SP Kingsworthy.

6 TL (no SP) and over small ford. At TJ, TR to Ovington. TL (no SP) opposite Lane End Cottages. Continue towards Avington. ***19.5km (12 miles)***

7 Arrive TJ and TL (no SP) to Avington. TR SP Easton/Winchester, and pass the entrance to Avington Park. ***24km (15 miles)***

8 At TJ (by The Cricketers) TL and take No Through Road. At XR, SO. ***26.5km (16.5 miles)***

9 Arrive M3 (29km/18 miles). Dismount and use pedestrian underpass to cross M3 to Winnall Industrial Estate. Descend hill and cross bridge.

10 At TJ TL, get into right hand lane and TR, SP City Centre. Follow one-way system to top of St. Georges Street.

11 TR at traffic lights into Jewry Street (ignore sign pointing left for station). At next traffic lights (by cycle shop) TL and at next XR (lights here too) either SO for station or TR for Worthy Lane and car park. ***33km (20.5 miles)***

Food and drink 

Winchester is well supplied with pubs and cafés – at the weekend try the Cathedral Close. There are no shops in the small villages on the route but Winchester and Alresford (see route 1) are well supplied. There are several pubs in Alresford. Pubs en route include:

Cart and Horses, Kings Worthy

The Trout, Itchen Abbas

White Swan Hotel, Alresford

Serves everything from cups of tea to full meals all day, and is popular with local cyclists.

Café Cresson, Alresford

Open daily throughout the week.

The Bush, Ovington

The Chestnut Horse, Easton

The Cricketers, Easton

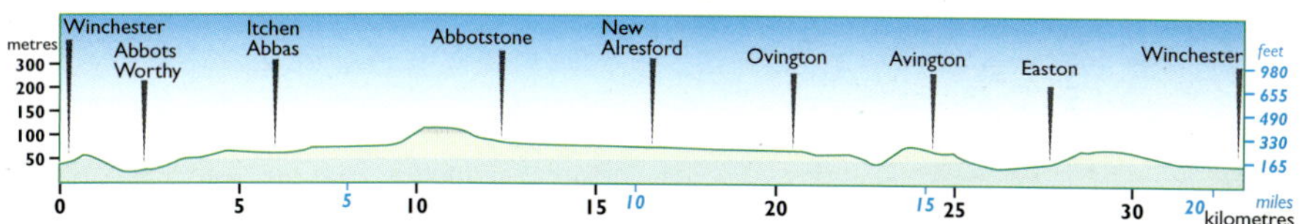

The River Arle at Old Alresford

Route **8**

LYTCHETT MINSTER AND WAREHAM FOREST

Route information

Distance 35km (21.5 miles)

Grade Moderate

Terrain An off-road ride through woods on well-surfaced bridleways.

Time to allow 4–5 hours.

Getting there by car Lytchett Minster is on the western outskirts of Poole and close to the A35. Roadside parking is usually possible. There is parking at the Courtyard Centre, but please be fair and don't park here all day if it's busy.

Getting there by train The nearest station, Hamworthy Junction, is on the main Waterloo to Weymouth line and has a frequent service. Telephone (0345) 484950.

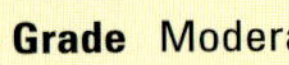

From Lytchett Minster for a few miles of country lanes and bridleway before launching into the Wareham Forest. Good firm bridleways and country lanes cross this quiet area of forest and heathland. The route passes through the hilltop village of Lytchett Matravers before finishing with a downhill run.

Places of interest along the route

A Courtyard Centre, Lytchett Minster

An arts and craft centre with numerous country crafts, gardens, garden centre and a Museum of Yesteryear. Picnic area and restaurant. Open all year (except Christmas week), daily 1000–1700. Admission free. Telephone (01202) 623423.

B Woolsbarrow Hill Fort

Dorset's smallest iron age earthwork, covering just 0.8ha (2 acres) and around 3000 years old. The site was later used as a Roman camp and has excellent views in all directions. Now covered with naturally seeded trees and only accessible by forest tracks, the site is generally quiet and deserted.

Food and drink

Dylans Restaurant, Courtyard Centre, Lytchett Minster

Licensed restaurant serving lunches and teas.

Rose and Crown, Lytchett Matravers

Local ales and bar snacks.

Country Lane, Dorset

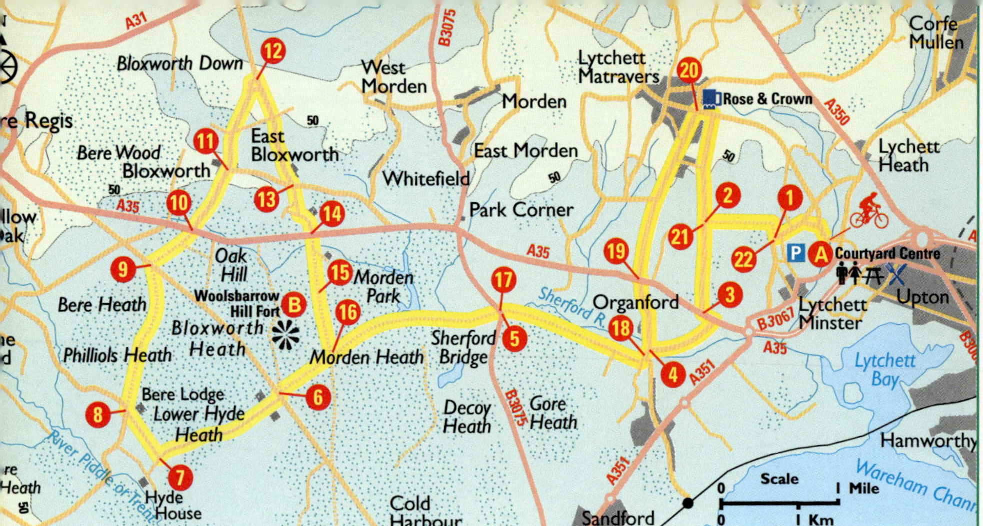

Route description 

Leave the Courtyard Centre and TL. After about 200 metres, TL again and follow road slightly up hill (past school on the left and houses on the right).

1 TR onto bridleway on the bend in road. Go through gate and follow bridleway around to left.

2 TL at minor road.

3 TL at junction with A35 (take great care) and TR at next junction, SP Organford.

4 TL at TJ and over the small bridge. TR on bridleway immediately after bridge. After 150 metres TR (SP Sherford Bridge) through green metal gate. SO on hardpack path. After 0.5km (0.3 mile) carry SO up through woods. Follow main bridleway to road at Sherford Bridge.

4km (2.5 miles)

5 Cross road and continue on bridleway (just to the left over cattlegrid), alongside hedge and through metal gate. Follow main bridleway through wooden posts marked with blue arrow. After about 2km (1 mile) where hardpack bridleways cross, carry SO. Follow track up hill and round to the left. Stay on this hardpack bridleway as it winds to junction with road.

6km (3.5 miles)

6 TL onto road and immediately TR onto bridleway, SP Hyde House. SO between buildings and stay on hardpack bridleway for approximately 2km (1 mile).

9.5km (6 miles)

7 TR (opposite white sign Hyde Beeches) and SO to meet road.

8 Keep to right past the house (Bere Lodge) and onto bridleway (marked with a blue arrow). SO through barrier and SO again (care here, do not go right). Follow the hardpack bridleway as it winds slightly uphill, eventually joining the road.

13km (8 miles)

9 SO onto next section of bridleway which continues to wind slightly uphill. After several hundred metres, the track divides, TL onto soft-pack route up between trees and SO to join A35.

10 Cross A35 with care and continue on minor road, SP Bloxworth, as it climbs gently.

11 TL at junction at top of hill and then follow road round to the right, down to foot of hill and up the other side.

12 TR (there is a small triangle of roads).

14.5km (9 miles)

13 At TJ at top of hill SO (across road) and onto bridleway. After 200 metres, SO onto bridleway (do not go right). Follow bridleway round to left (past houses on left) then round to right to meet the A35.

14 Cross A35 onto bridleway. After about 100 metres cross small ford (or use the bridge to left). Take narrow bridleway immediately to the right (do not go SO towards buildings) up through the trees, up sandy hill, round to right and past several large wooden posts. Follow the bridleway around to the left, slightly uphill, eventually reaching junction with hardpack bridleway.

15 TL at junction and, after about 100 metres, SO to sandy hill in distance, (not left down hardpack bridleway). Go down other side of hill. After about 200 meteres SO across another bridleway (which comes from right and then goes sharp left). SO here following blue arrow on post.

16 After a few 100 metres, another bridleway crosses your route. TL here, down hardpack bridleway by SP Woolsbarrow Hill Fort. Follow bridleway around to right and downhill. SO where bridleways cross. Stay on this main bridleway passing wooden posts, round to right and then left up through woods past pylon on right. Continue through trees, passing metal gate on right, then through next metal gate (across bridleway) and follow tracks SO to road at Sherford Bridge.

17 SO across road to bridleway opposite, through barrier and SO (not right). SO again onto softpack bridleway (do not carry on round to right on bend down hardpack). Cycle up through woods and eventually on to hardpack bridleway, through green metal gate and round to left to join road at small bridge.

23km (14.5 miles)

18 TL onto road and over small bridge. Follow SP to Lytchett Matravers, to A35.

19 SO A35 at staggered XR.

20 TR at XR, by Rose & Crown. After 150 metres, TR into Foxhills Road, then TL at next junction (staying on Foxhills Road with Foxhills estate on right). ***31km (19 miles)***

21 TL along bridleway and through avenue of trees, follow onto junction with road.

22 TL and retrace route to the Courtyard Centre and the end of the route.

35km (21.5 miles)

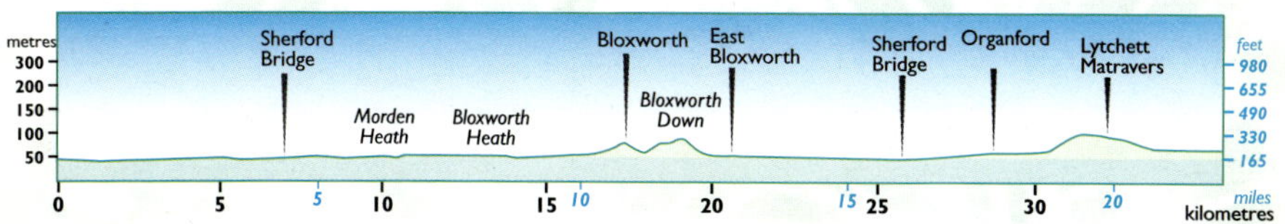

Route 9

WICKHAM, WEST MEON AND OLD WINCHESTER HILL

Route information

Distance 35.5km (22 miles)

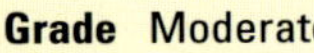

Grade Moderate

Terrain From Wickham along a cycle trail on the bed of a disused railway. The surface is mostly firm and smooth but can become muddy after prolonged periods of rain. Just one significant climb between West Meon and Old Winchester Hill, and from there the route is mostly downhill back to Wickham.

Time to allow 2½–3 hours.

Getting there by car Wickham lies at the junction of the A32 (Alton to Fareham road) and the A334 from Southampton. Parking in the centre of Wickham is time restricted but there is a free car park signed from the town centre.

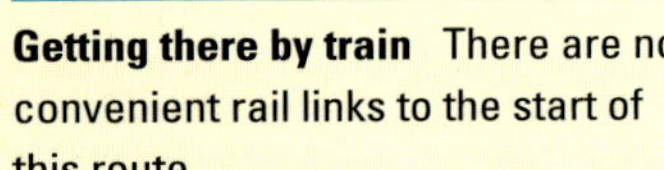

Getting there by train There are no convenient rail links to the start of this route.

Places of interest along the route

A West Meon

In addition to the pub named after him, West Meon churchyard contains the grave of Thomas Lord, founder of Lords cricket ground. Also buried here, a man whose behaviour was not cricket – the spy Guy Burgess.

B Old Winchester Hill

A National Nature Reserve and Site of Special Scientific Interest. The 60ha (160 acres) are owned by English Nature. The hill, a local landmark, overlooks the Meon Valley and on a fine day there are magnificent views across to the Isle of Wight. The site contains an Iron Age hill fort, downland, woodland and is home to orchids and rare plants – the summit of the route both literally and figuratively.

C Soberton Station, near Droxford

A plaque close to the former site of Soberton Station records that Winston Churchill's train was stationed in a siding nearby, prior to the D Day landings on 6 June 1944.

Food and drink

There are numerous cafés and pubs in Wickham.

Hurdlers, Droxford

Conveniently placed for both the outward and return journey.

Red Lion, West Meon

Real ales and bar snacks.

Thomas Lord, West Meon

Real ales, bar snacks and restaurant.

Hampshire countryside

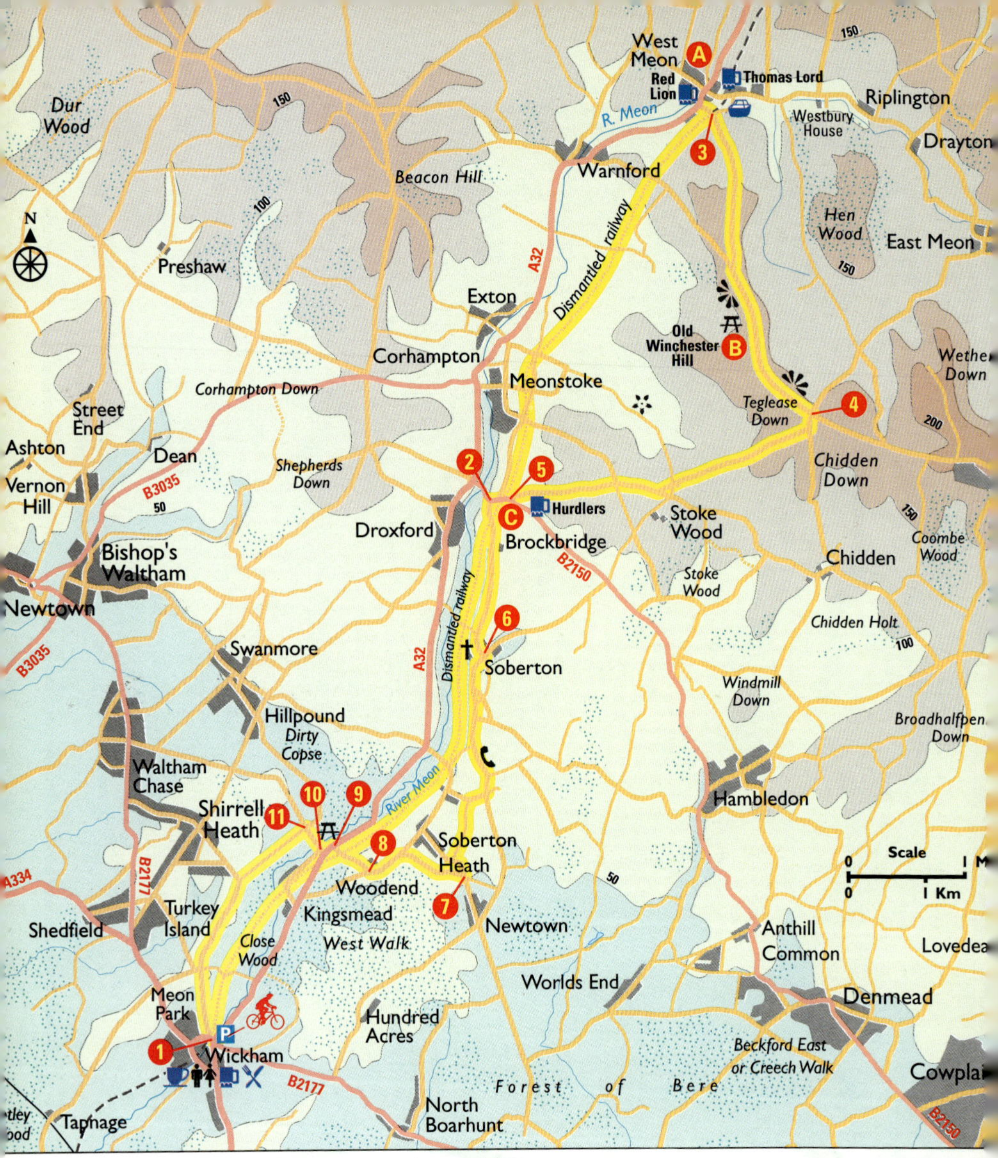

West Meon
A
Thomas Lord
Red Lion
R. Meon
Riplington
Westbury House
Drayton
Dur Wood
150
Beacon Hill
Warnford
3
Hen Wood
East Meon
100
Preshaw
A32
Dismantled railway
150
Exton
Old Winchester Hill
B
Wether Down
Corhampton
Meonstoke
Teglease Down
4
200
Corhampton Down
Street End
Ashton
Dean
Shepherds Down
2
5
Chidden Down
Vernon Hill
B3035
50
Droxford
C
Hurdlers
Stoke Wood
150
Coombe Wood
Brockbridge
Bishop's Waltham
B2150
Chidden
Stoke Wood
Newtown
Dismantled railway
6
Chidden Holt
B3035
Swanmore
A32
Soberton
100
Windmill Down
Hillpound
Dirty Copse
Broadhalfpen Down
River Meon
Waltham Chase
10
9
Hambledon
Shirrell Heath
11
8
Soberton Heath
Scale
0
1 M
A334
B2177
50
0
1 Km
Woodend
7
Turkey Island
Kingsmead
Newtown
Anthill Common
Shedfield
Close Wood
West Walk
Lovedean
Worlds End
Meon Park
Hundred Acres
Denmead
P
1
Wickham
Beckford East or Creech Walk
Cowplain
B2177
Forest of Bere
North Boarhunt
Tapnage
B2150

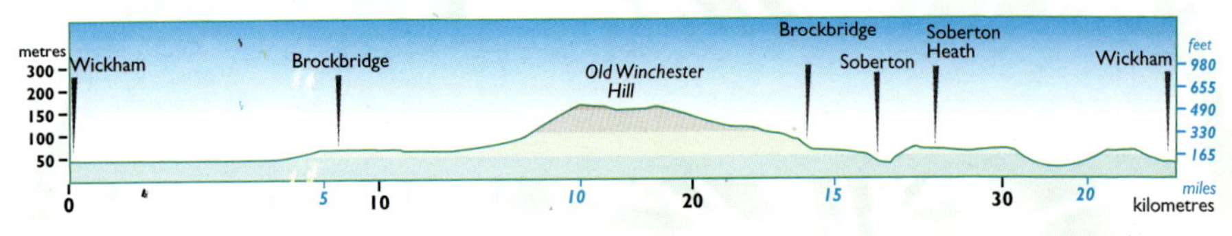

Route description

The signed car park in Wickham is in Station Close at the start of the cycle trail.

1 Leave the car park and join the trail by the bridge over the River Meon. Head north. After rain the first 0.5km (0.3 miles) can be difficult, but carry on as the going gets much easier. Continue along cycle trail.

2 After 9km (5.5 miles) the trail crosses the Droxford road. It is possible to leave the trail here to either visit the Hurdlers and/or join the return route for a shorter ride, in which case retrace your route to Wickham or TR onto B2150, SP Soberton, and continue the route from direction 5. Otherwise, continue along cycle trail. Between this point on the trail and West Meon, two bridges are missing and the trail descends from the embankment to cross byroads.

3 From the SP Access to West Meon, descend to Station Road. To visit West Meon, TL and at TJ TR onto A32 and into village. Return to Station Road to pick up the route. Otherwise, TR and climb the route's only hill. At TJ, TL for Old Winchester Hill (19km/12 miles). The entrance to Old Winchester Hill is about 1km (0.3 mile) on the right. ***15km (9.5 miles)***

4 At XR, TR SP Droxford, Hambledon and Corehampton. After around 0.1km, follow road around to right (no SP) and descend towards Droxford. ***21.5km (13.5 miles)***

5 At TJ, TR onto B2150, then TL (Station Road), SP Soberton. If you wish, you can rejoin the cycle trail here and retrace your route to Wickham. The D Day plaque is on a postbox about 100m from the turn.

26.5km (16.5 miles)

6 TR at XR, SP Soberton Heath, Newtown and Southwick. ***29km (18 miles)***

7 At staggered XR TR into Liberty Road, SP Woodend (32km/20 miles). Then at TJ TL, no SP.

8 TR SP Swanmore and Curdridge.

9 At junction with A32, TL SP Wickham.

33.5km (21 miles)

10 TR SP Swanmore and Curdridge. The banks of the River Meon are on the right hand side of the road – a popular spot for picnics and paddling.

11 At XR, TL SP Wickham. Where the road bears right, TL into Mill Lane and return to the start of the route in Wickham.

35.5km (22 miles)

Route 10

ABBOTSBURY, CHESIL BEACH AND HARDY'S MONUMENT

Route information

Distance 37.5km (23.5 miles)

Grade Strenuous

Terrain Grassy downland, mostly unclassified minor roads, a section of old railway track and a rough beach road.

Time to allow 2–4 hours.

Getting there by car Martinstown can be reached from Dorchester by taking the B3150 west and at the roundabout with the bypass taking the second exit onto a minor road. From the west, RHF off the A35 at Winterbourne Abbas. Parking in the long single street of Martinstown is usually possible.

Getting there by train The nearest railway station is in Dorchester. Telephone (0345) 484950 for information.

From Martinstown to the sea, taking a rough beach road along Chesil Beach before heading back inland through the sleepy picturesque villages of Litton Cheney and the Bredys. After Littlebredy, the route climbs high up to the site of Hardy's Monument before the final exhilarating downhill run back to Martinstown. Note that sea weather conditions can be very different to those only a short distance inland – do not use the beach road in adverse weather, particularly if there is sea mist or fog.

Places of interest along the route

A Abbotsbury Swannery, Abbotsbury

One of the last examples of a managed swannery with hundreds of free flying swans, this swannery is over 600 years old. Cygnets hatch from late May to the end of June and this is the only place in the world where the public can access this event. Well signed from the road, a trip to the Swannery will mean a detour of about 5km (3 miles). Restaurant, gift shop and visitor centre. Open daily March to October 1000–1800. Charge. Telephone (01305) 871858. The **Tithe Barn Children's Farm**, home to farm animals and a working dovecote, adjoins the Swannery. Charge. Telephone (01305) 871817 for information.

B Sub Tropical Gardens, Abbotsbury

The gardens comprise over 8ha (20 acres) of woodland valley. Magnificent 18th-century walled garden, rare and exotic plants, lily ponds, peacocks and pheasants. Tea garden and gift shop. Open all year, daily 1000–dusk. Charge. Telephone (01305) 871387.

C Hardy's Monument

Monument to Admiral Hardy, of *Kiss me Hardy* fame, as Nelson lay dying on the deck of *HMS Victory*. This monument commands spectacular 360 degree panoramic views and has been restored so that visitors can climb to the top. Open at all reasonable times. Admission free.

Chesil Beach

Food and drink

Brewers Arms, Martinstown
Local ales and bar meals.

Kings Arms, Portesham
Bar meals and restaurant.

Wheelwrights Tearooms, Abbotsbury
Cream teas, homemade soups and light lunches.

Old Schoolhouse Tearoom, Abbotsbury
Cream teas and light lunches.

Beach Café, West Bexington
Sandwiches, pies and ice cream. Closed December to February.

Manor Hotel, West Bexington
Free house. Cream teas and outside seating in the garden.

Route description

Leave Martinstown to the east on the B3159, SP Upwey. Climb the hill and down the other side.

1 TR just after the Upwey village sign, SP Coryates & Portesham. Take care as this is a sharp turn on a fast descent. ***4.5km (3 miles)***

2 TR SP Waddon & Portesham.

3 TL at TJ, SP Portesham, and down through village. At TJ by Kings Arms TR, SP Abbotsbury. ***10.5km (6.5 miles)***

4 TR after Millmead Hotel onto track SP Evershot Farm. At house on right, keep SO downhill. At foot (in farmyard) TR and up onto wide bridleway.

5 SO through gate. Bridleway becomes narrower here for a short distance, then opens up again and passes a ruined chapel on the left and then an old engine shed on the right. **11.5km (7 miles)**

6 TR and rejoin road at Abbotsbury. Follow road through centre of village. Diversion to left to visit the Swannery (well signposted).

7 TL SP Sub Tropical Gardens and Chesil Beach. Warning – in rough weather (particularly with sea fog), do not take the coast road, instead TR and tackle the tough climb of Abbotsbury Hill, followed by superb high speed freewheel and rejoin the route at direction 10.

8 TR at mini-roundabout at the shore and follow the beach road. The condition of this

Abbotsbury

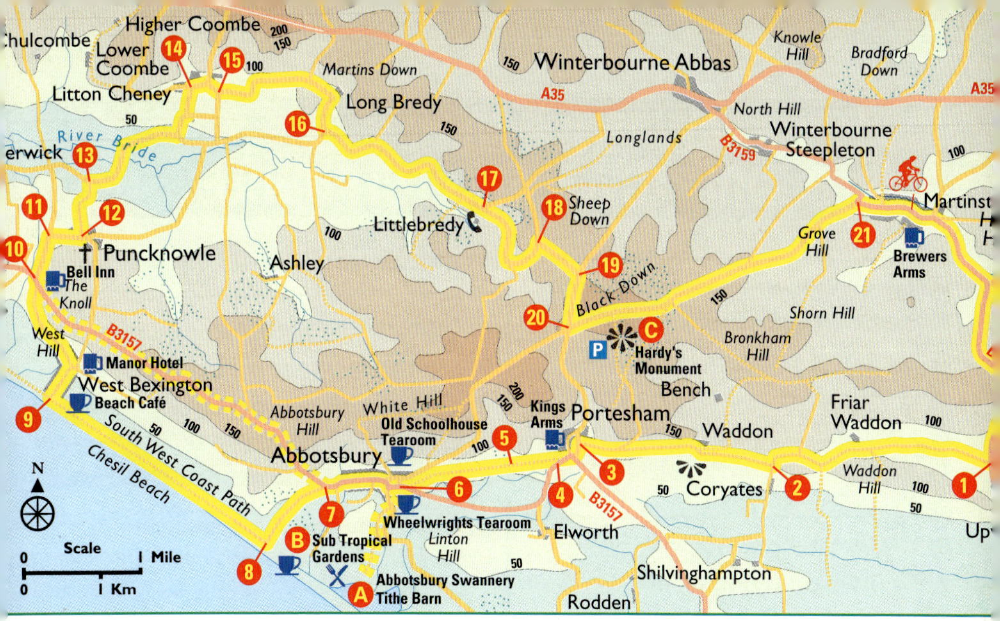

road varies from well surfaced, to rough and potholed to becoming covered in beach pebbles close to West Bexington. In places the pebbles are deep so take care not to hit these patches too fast. ***15km (9.5 miles)***

9 TR and climb hill through West Bexington. ***19km (12 miles)***

10 TL at TJ (Bell Inn opposite) no SP, and then TR SP Puncknowle. Take care – traffic comes down this road at high speed. ***21km (13 miles)***

11 TR SP Puncknowle.

12 TL just before church and go down through the village. No SP. ***22km (13.5 miles)***

13 TR SP Litton Cheney and follow through the village. ***22.5km (14 miles)***

14 TR SP Long Bredy.

15 Keep left, no SP, and pass through Long Bredy. ***25km (15.5 miles)***

16 TL, SP Littlebredy.

17 TR at telephone box, no SP. This road gives terrific views of a sweeping parkland and then rounds a few cottages to present the real start of the climb up. ***29.5km (18.5 miles)***

18 Take RHF, no SP. ***31km (19 miles)***

19 TR at TJ, SP Hardy's Monument.

20 TL at XR, SP Hardy's Monument. Look for the monument at the summit of the hill. Pause to see the view or climb the tower, before cycling down to Martinstown.

21 TR into Martinstown and the finish of the route. ***37.5km (23.5 miles)***

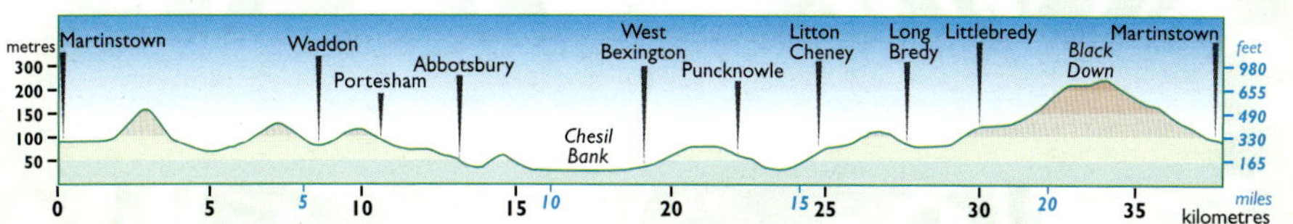

Route 11

THE LAWRENCE TRAIL – PUDDLETOWN AND TOLPUDDLE

Route information

Distance 40km (25 miles)

Grade Easy

Terrain Quiet and mostly flat country lanes.

Time to allow 2–4 hours.

Getting there by car Wareham can be reached by the A35/A351 from Poole in the east and by the A352 from Dorchester in the west. There are signed car parks in the town but use the long-term car park in Streche Road, off West Street.

Getting there by train Wareham is on the main Waterloo to Weymouth line and has a frequent service. Telephone (0345) 484950 for information.

From Wareham across the causeway of the River Frome watermeadow (which gives Purbeck its island character). On through the flat wooded lanes of the Frome valley to Wool and a complete change of scenery through Bovington, a quite unexpected conurbation with plenty of military hardware on all sides and vast wide, but quiet roads. Leave along King George V Avenue, the road where T.E. Lawrence was killed. The route continues along an unsurfaced road to cross the Frome by the picturesque village of Morton. An optional additional section to Tincleton and Tolpuddle is offered (adding 11km/7 miles). Back to Wareham through the picture postcard villages on the Piddle valley. There are three fords on this route, but don't worry, all have small bridges alongside. There are no significant hills.

Places of interest along the route

A Tank Museum, Bovington

HQ of the Royal Armoured Corps. Thousands of artefacts and over 300 vehicles from 27 countries. T.E. Lawrence was stationed here at the time of his death and there is a small exhibit to him in the museum. Free Tank Firepower and Mobility displays July to September. Gift shop and restaurant. Open all year, daily 1000–1700. Charge. Telephone (01929) 405096.

B Clouds Hill

T.E. Lawrence, otherwise known as Lawrence of Arabia, bought this cottage in 1925 and used it as a retreat from army life. He wrote *The Seven Pillars of Wisdom* here. It is preserved much as he left it, with furniture that he designed, and his books and typewriter. Lawrence had a fatal motorcycle accident 400 yards from this cottage and is buried in Moreton churchyard. National Trust property. Open April to November, Wednesday–Friday and Sunday 1200–1700. Charge. Telephone (01929) 405616.

C St Nicholas Church, Morton

After his accident, Lawrence was taken to Bovington Military Hospital, but died six days later. He is buried in the small churchyard at Moreton, entered by a covered lych gate. The mourners included Winston Churchill, Mrs Thomas Hardy, Augustus John and Siegfried Sassoon. Always open. Admission free.

D Tolpuddle Martyrs Museum, Tolpuddle

Located in the TUC cottages. In 1834, six agricultural labourers were sentenced to seven years' transportation to Australia for rebelling against a cut in their wages. This action saw the start of the trade unions. After public outcry, the labourers were pardoned and returned to England. In 1934 the TUC built six cottages in Tolpuddle in memory of the martyrs. Open all year, daily 1100–1700. Admission free.

E St Martins Church, Wareham

A little Saxon Church at the north end of the town in which there is a life size effigy of Lawrence of Arabia carved by his friend Eric Kennington. It shows Lawrence in Arab dress surrounded by his dearest possessions. Usually open but if closed, request key from the Tourist Information Office. Admission free.

F Wareham Museum

The museum in East Street has a large display of Lawrence memorabilia. Open all year, Monday–Saturday 1000–1300 and 1400–1700. Admission free.

Food and drink

Wareham has numerous pubs, cafés and tearooms. The Anglebury Coffee House, North Street, has a corner seat with a small plate saying that Lawrence used to sit there.

Rose Mullion Tearooms, Wool
Morning coffee, lunches and cream teas.

Beehive Café, Bovington
Breakfasts, lunches and light meals.

Barry's Bistro, Elles Road, Bovington
Light meals.

Moreton Post Office
Icecream and drinks.

Martyrs Inn, Tolpuddle
Local ales and excellent food.

Route description

From the car park, turn into West Street and TR at the traffic lights into South Street. SO across South Bridge on the B3075 and cross the flat reedy land of the Causeway.

1 TR SP Creech, Steeple, for a short distance and then cross the bypass (with care – staggered crossing), still SP Creech & Steeple.

2 TR by the Country Hotel, SP East Holme.

3 At XR SO, SP Wool (Holme Lane). Much of the land in this area is owned by the military and is used for exercises – you will see red flags and gunnery stations. Continue to Wool.
5km (3 miles)

4 TR SP Dorchester and Weymouth. TR and cross the railway line. Take second left turning to cross Woolbridge. Stop to read the inscription, warning of the dangers of deportation for damaging the bridge.
11km (7 miles)

5 TL SP Bovington. Bovington Road is very wide (for military purposes) and passes the Tank Museum on the right. The road leaves the town and becomes King George V Avenue.

6 Pass Clouds Hill on the right. At TJ just after Clouds Hill, TL SP Tincleton and Dorchester. ***16km (10 miles)***

7 TL at XR (unsurfaced road known as Moreton Drive).

8 Cross the ford at Moreton. It is possible to ride across if you are bold enough. If you use the bridge, dismount and walk as this is a footpath. ***18.5km (11.5 miles)***

9 TR SP Dorchester and Weymouth (do not take the right turn by the Post Office as this is a deadend). Almost immediately RHF. No SP, but Glebe Farm is on your right hand.

10 TR onto the B3390, SP Affpuddle and Bere Regis. Cross the old Hurst Bridges and then watch out for the Kissing Robots sculpture in front of the factory unit.

20km (12.5 miles)

11 At XR SO to follow the standard route to direction 12.

To follow the optional section of route take LHF, SP Dorchester. NB: only use the on-road part of this optional route after the new Puddletown bypass is open (scheduled for Spring/Summer 1999). HGVs make the present A35 extremely dangerous to cycle along, as it is very narrow here. Using the off-road section avoids this problem altogether.

a LHF SP Dorchester immediately after the robots.

b TR SP Puddletown and keep straight on to direction (c) for the on-road route, or to follow the off-road route:

(i) TR to Admiston Farm and go up the concreted driveway.

(ii) Bridleway splits to a gate on the right, ignore this, and go through the next metal gate on the right. Bridleway runs uphill through the middle of the field to the metal gate at the far end. Through this and uphill a little more into the woods before dropping down (through two gates) almost to the junction with the A35.

(iii) TR onto bridleway.

(iv) SO across road and continue route at direction e.

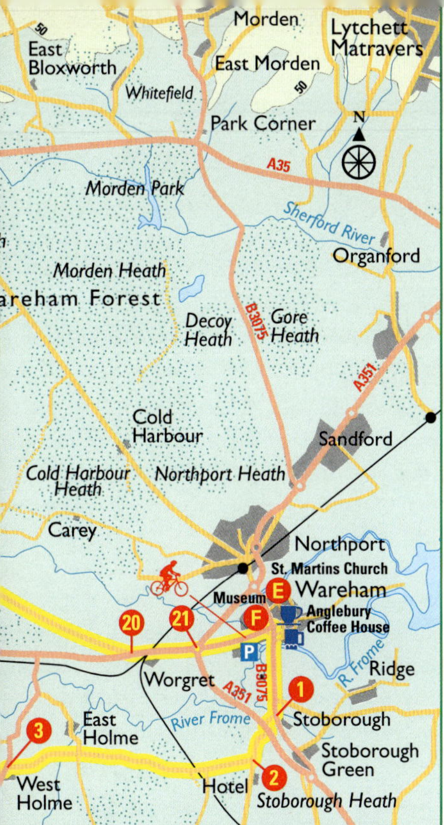

c TR, SP Tolpuddle. The Tolpuddle Martyrs Museum is on the left after 3km (2 miles).

d TR (sharp turn after dropping down to village) SP Southover and Affpuddle. Pass over river and then TL.

e TR SP Moreton and continue the route at direction 12, except SO SP Briantspuddle.

12 TR SP Briantspuddle. Note the war memorial and street of cottages on the right.
24km (15 miles)

13 SO SP Throop ***25km (15.5 miles)***

14 TL on gravel road at sharp right hand bend. Note that there is no SP here. This short section fords the River Piddle in two places (with bridges too). TR after the second ford to join the tarmac road.
26km (16 miles)

15 TL SP Bere Regis and go uphill to direction 16. Alternatively, to avoid hill and take short cut:

f SO onto unmade road.

g SO at XR SP Lane End & Culeaze. Rejoin route at direction 18 except TR here, SP Hyde.

16 TR SP Bovington & Wool.

17 TL SP Hyde.

18 SO, SP Hyde. This road turns and crosses the River Piddle and then climbs a little by the golf course. ***29.5km (18.5 miles)***

19 TL SP Worgret and Wareham. Little remains of the heathlands that were Hardy's Egdon Heath, but the scrub land by this road gives some idea of its nature. This long straight road drops imperceptibly downhill and offers the chance of a really fast run if so inclined.
34km (21 miles)

20 TL onto A352, taking care.

21 SO at roundabout to return to Wareham to the finish. This means crossing the traffic flow on the bypass so take care.
40km (25 miles)

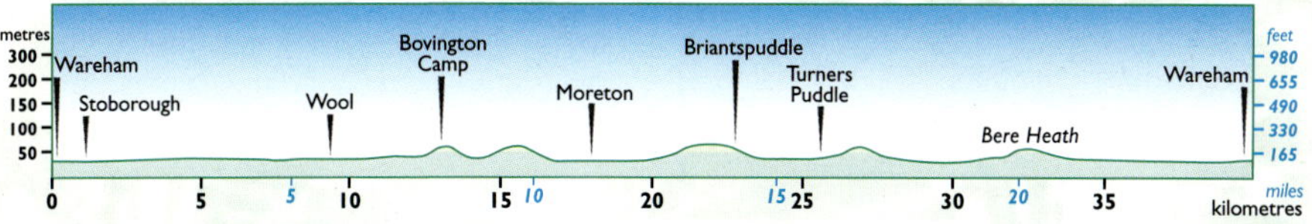

Route 12 ISLE OF WIGHT – EASTERN LOOP

Route information

Distance 40km (25 miles)

Grade Moderate

Terrain The route avoids main roads and major hills, although there are a couple of short steep hills, which may be easily walked. The optional route to Ashey Down has a strenuous climb. The initial downhill section of the second optional route, after Downend, should be treated with care.

Time to allow 2½–3 hours, but could easily make a day ride.

Getting there by car Portsmouth is on the M27 and is easily accessible from all directions. There are regular passenger and car ferry sailings between Portsmouth and Ryde. Cycles may be carried on the catamaran (passenger ferry). Telephone (0990) 827744 for ferry information. Portsmouth has several multi-storey car parks and there is a car park near the ferry terminals.

Getting there by train There are regular services to Portsmouth Harbour Station, close to the ferry terminals. Telephone (0345) 484950 for information.

Places of interest along the route

A Brading

Once a busy port, Brading now has plenty to offer the visitor. **Lilliput Museum of Antique Dolls and Toys** has over 2000 exhibits, ranging from an Egyptian grave figure to a Matrestika Doll presented by the Soviet premier Krushchev. Open daily, April to September 0930–2130; October to March 1000–1700. Charge. Telephone (01983) 407231. **Nunwell House**, set in fine parkland and gardens, reflects five centuries of island history. Open end June to September (closed during early August), Monday–Wednesday 1300–1700. Telephone (01983) 407240. The **Isle of Wight Waxworks Museum** illustrates over 2000 years of history with figures, sound and light. Open May to September, daily 1000–2200; October to April 1000–1700. Charge. Telephone (01983) 407286. On the outskirts of Brading, **Morton Manor** was originally built in 1249. View the house and award-winning gardens, winery and maze. Open Easter to October, Monday–Friday and Sunday 1000–1730. Charge. Telephone (01983) 406168. The **Roman Villa** has fine mosaic floors. Open March to November, daily 1000–1700. Charge. Telephone (01983) 406223.

B Godshill

A charming village of thatch-roofed cottages. The **Old Smithy and Gardens** contain landscaped flower gardens, a herb garden, grottos and aviaries. Gift shops and restaurant. Shops open all year, daily 0900–1700. Gardens open March to October, daily 0900–1700. Charge for admission to gardens. Telephone (01983)

840364. The **Toy Museum** contains around 2000 toys, models, games and dolls. Open May to October, daily (except Saturdays in October) 1000–1700. Charge. Telephone (01983) 840181.

C Arreton Manor

Believed to be left by Alfred the Great to his son Etherward. Now mainly Jacobean architecture with fine panelling and furniture. Wireless museum and collection of fabric, lace and costume. Open all year, Monday–Friday 1000–1700, Sunday 1200–1700. Charge. Telephone (01983) 528134.

D Robin Hill Country Park

Comprising 35ha (88 acres) of countryside with assault course, reptile house and many animals and birds. Café. Open all year, daily 1000–1700. Charge. Telephone (01983) 527352.

E Isle of Wight Steam Railway

A collection of restored locomotives and rolling stock with a museum of the island's railway history. Steam trains run between Wootton and Smallbrook Junction (7.5km/5 miles). Open on selected days March to December. Charge. Telephone (01983) 882204.

F Brickfields Horse Country

Shire horse centre with guided tours, parades and demonstrations. Open all year, daily 1000–1700. Telephone (01983) 566801.

Godshill

Route description 

At the end of Ryde Pier TL. Then, TR at mini roundabout into Dover Street. At TJ (top of Dover Street) TR into Park Road, which becomes Star Street. Then TL into High Street (one way system) and continue out of Ryde.

1 TL, SP Ashey and Newchurch. At XR, SO.

2 TL into Green Lane, SP Nunwell, Brading and Sandown. Continue towards Brading and direction 3. ***4.5km (3 miles)***

For an optional route to Brading, continue SO.

a At top of hill, TL, SP Brading, Bembridge and Sandown. Descend steep hill with care.

b At TJ, TL towards Brading. At junction with A3055 in Brading, TR and continue to Yardbridge XR and direction 4.

3 Arrive TJ with A3055. TR into Brading and continue through town. ***7km (4.5 miles)***

4 At Yardbridge XR, TR and then TL into Lower Adgestone Road, SP Adgestone and Alverstone. Continue, passing Morton Manor and Roman Villa.

5 TR (at cycleway sign). Then, at TJ, TL and continue towards Winford.

6 Arrive Winford. TR into Forest Road, following cycleway sign. ***13.5km (8.5 miles)***

7 At staggered XR, SO, SP Arreton and Newport. Then at TJ, TL SP Godshill and Newport. Continue over A3056, towards Sandford.

8 Arrive TJ with A3020. TR, SP Godshill and continue through Godshill.

9 TL, SP Chale and Ventnor (19.5km/ 12 miles). Then TR SP Chale.

10 At top of hill, TR into Bagwich Lane, no SP (22.5km/14 miles). Then TR, no SP.

11 At A3020, TL then immediate TR, SP Merstone.

12 Arrive TJ with A3056. TR, then TL, SP Cowes.

13 To follow main route: SO then TR, no SP. Continue past Robin Hill Country Park.

For optional route on bridleway, TR and after 250m, TL onto track (good surface but initial descent is steep). Continue to road where TR (direction 15) to rejoin route.

14 TR, no SP.

Food and drink

Refreshments are available at Portsmouth Harbour Station. Note that no refreshments can be obtained on the passenger ferry (fast crossing), but Ryde has a good supply of shops, cafés and pubs. Brading also has several tea-rooms and pubs, and a convenience store.

Bugle Inn, Brading
Pub dating back to 1314. Bar meals.

Cask and Taveners, Godshill
Pub and restaurant, with garden.

Willow Tree, Godshill
Teas, coffees and snacks. Garden.

Hare and Hounds, Arreton
Pub and restaurant.

15 Continue SO, through Havenstreet. At XR, SO, SP Binstead and Ryde. ***35.5km (22 miles)***

16 TL for Brickfields Horse Country, or SO to continue route.

17 At XR, TL, SP Ryde. Follow SP to town centre and esplanade, to return to Ryde pier. ***40km (25 miles)***

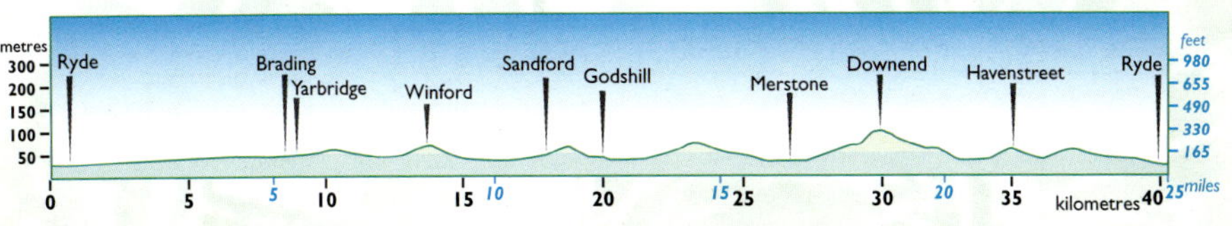

Route 13

WEYMOUTH AND PORTLAND BILL

Route information

Distance 40km (25 miles)

Grade Strenuous

Terrain This route takes you through Weymouth, along rural lanes and rugged coastline. Mostly left turns on the busy roads avoid traffic problems. There are hilly suburban roads with some steep gradients, but with fabulous views.

Time to allow 3–4 hours.

Getting there by car Weymouth can be reached on the A354 from Dorchester to the north, from Wareham on the A352/A353 from the east, and from Bridport on the B3157 from the west. There are many car parks in the town but for this ride try for the Swannery Car Park, by Swannery Bridge off the Kings Roundabout and Radipole Park Drive.

Getting there by train Weymouth is the terminus of the main Waterloo line and has a frequent service. There is a regular through train service from the Midlands. There is also a service from Bristol, via Yeovil Junction. Telephone (0345) 484950 for information.

The route leaves Weymouth Esplanade by the Clock Tower and threads its way along the seafront to the quay, over the bridge to Brewers Quay, before heading off to the Isle of Portland. A big climb with hairpin bends leads to the top of the island from where unexpectedly wide roads lead down through Easton and out to Portland Bill, before returning back through Weston. On returning to the mainland, the route takes narrow lanes around the north of Weymouth, largely avoiding the town, to return along a cycleway overlooking Radipole Lake Nature Reserve.

Places of interest along the route

A Weymouth

Weymouth is a busy holiday town at all times of the year. The complex of narrow streets of the town centre is worth exploring. The painted Clock Tower on the Esplanade is a prominent landmark and from here on clear days the chalk figure of King George III can be seen on White Horse Hill to the northeast. **Brewers Quay**, the site of the Devenish Brewery in the old harbour area, has been restored and contains craft stalls, speciality shops, pubs and cafés. Also in the centre is **Weymouth Museum**, which describes the town's maritime history and has changing exhibits; the **Timewalk**, which has 19 life-like scenes recreating the sights, sounds and smells of 600 years of Weymouth's history; and the **Devenish Story** is about the brewery sited here. **Discovery** is a hands-on multi-media science attraction. Brewers Quay is open all year (except Christmas and the last two weeks of January), daily 0930–1700; Easter and May spring Bank Holiday weekends, and during school summer holidays 0930–2130. Charge for attractions. Telephone (01305) 766880. **Nothe Fort**, a Museum of Coastal Defence, was built between 1860 and 1872. There are more than 30 displays and dioramas with models, photographs and exhibits illustrating service life in the fort, its history and the part played by Weymouth during World War II. Open May to September, daily 1030–1730; Sundays and Bank Holidays 1400–1730; summer and autumn school half-term 1400–1730. Charge. Telephone (01305) 787243/786025. The **Tudor House**, by Brewers Quay, was originally built between 1570 and 1603 and has been restored and furnished in the style of the 17th century. Open June to September, Tuesday–Friday 1100–1545; October to May, first Sunday of each month 1400–1600. Charge. Telephone (01305) 812341/788168.

B Isle of Portland

Portland is a true island but for the sand bar of Chesil Beach. The size of the stones in Chesil are graded from Portland to Abbotsbury and with experience it is possible to determine exactly how far along the beach you are. Just off the route, Castletown is a lively centre for diving with pubs, café and hotel. **Portland Castle**, run by English Heritage, was one of Henry VIII's chain of defensive fortresses and built in 1539. It was operational until 1954. Themed weekends throughout the summer. Open April to October, daily 1000–1800. Charge (includes taped tour). Telephone (01305) 820539.

C Portland Museum and Shipwreck Museum, Wakeham

Founded by Marie Stopes in 1930, the museum is located in two thatched cottages, one of which was used by Thomas Hardy in *The Well-Beloved*. Exhibitions on shipwrecks, smuggling and Portland's natural and social history. Picnic area and gift shop. Open Easter to October, daily 1030–1300 and 1330–1700. Charge. Telephone (01305) 821804.

D Portland Bill and Lighthouse

Portland Bill and Chesil Beach are the sites of strong currents and many shipwrecks. The lighthouse guides vessels heading for Portland and Weymouth, and serves as a waymark for ships in the English Channel. Originally constructed during the 18th century, the lighthouse was demanned in 1996 and is now operated automatically. Open to the public most days (telephone for details). Visitors can climb right up to the lamp. Charge. Telephone (01305) 861233.

E Bennetts Water Gardens, Chickerell

The national collection of over 100 varieties of water lilies displayed within 2.5ha (6 acres) of natural lakes. Tropical house. Tearoom, plant and gift shop. Open April to August, Tuesday–Sunday 1000–1700; September, Tuesday–Saturday 1000–1700; October, Tuesday–Friday, 1000–1700. Charge. Telephone (01305) 785150.

Route description 

Leave the Clock Tower and head south, keeping the beach on your left until within sight of the Pavilion theatre.

1 Turn sharp right into one way street, marked Esplanade, then immediate TL into Pilgrims Way and immediate TR onto the quay road. Watch out for the railway lines!

2 Just before quay, road runs under bridge. TR at Royal Oak into St Marys Street. TL into Edmunds Street, then TL St Thomas Street and over the Town Bridge. TL immediately after bridge (Trinity Road) and along the other side, turning right into the Brewer's Quay area.

3 Cut through Spring Road and climb Rodwell Avenue.

4 TL at traffic lights onto A354.

5 At roundabout, keep left and head downhill for Portland, over Ferry Bridge and along the causeway. ***4km (2.5 miles)***

6 At Victoria Square keep left, climbing and following the A354 (9km/5.5 miles). To visit Castletown and Portland Castle, TL on first hairpin bend by Victoria Gardens.

7 TL (Verne Hill Road). Keep on climbing and the views begin to make it all worthwhile. Follow road as it turns sharp right at the top and runs along the ridge to the Portland Heights Hotel. Head for Easton. ***11km (7 miles)***

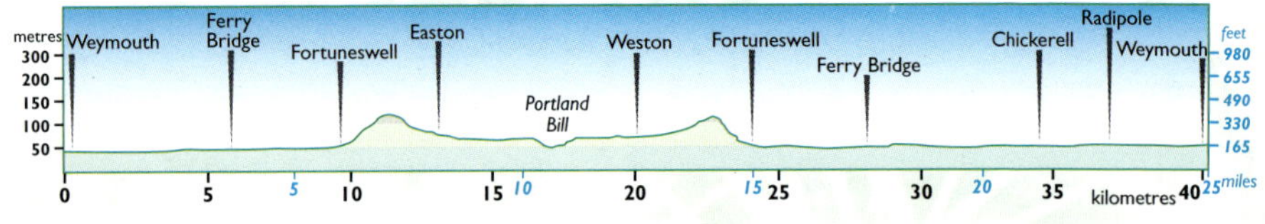

8 TL into Easton Lane, SP Easton. Travel gently downhill through the wide street passing the Portland Museum on your left.

14km (8.5 miles)

9 Keep left into Southwell Road

10 TL (onto Portland Bill Road) by the Eight Kings pub and head out to the lighthouse (15km/9.5 miles) before retracing to this point where TL for Weston. ***20km (12.5 miles)***

11 TL by St Georges Church (Wide Street) and back towards the Portland Heights Hotel.

12 TL, SP Weymouth & Fortuneswell A354, continue around the hairpin bend and downhill. Take in the view across Chesil Beach. Follow the one-way system through Fortuneswell and head back along the causeway.

25km (15.5 miles)

13 Keep left at Fords Corner, SP Bridport and Chickerell. ***30km (18.5 miles)***

14 TL at TJ into Wyke Road, SP Bridport.

15 TL into Chickerell Road at traffic lights. Pass the Swiss Cottage pub and the Land Registry Offices.

16 TR, SP Water Gardens and pass the gardens on your left.

17 At TJ, TR into Putton Lane.

18 TR, SP Radipole and Weymouth, and head down narrow lane. ***34.5km (21.5 miles)***

Food and drink

Weymouth has more restaurants and cafés than you can count. For basic fare, near the Clock Tower start of the ride, try the cycle-friendly Royal Crescent Restaurant.

Lobster Pot Café, Royal Manor Café and Cosy Café, Portland Bill
Teas, ice-cream, hot dogs and fish and chips.

Pulpit Inn, Portland Bill
Bar food, restaurant and accommodation.

Tea Cabin, Chesil Beach
Teas and snacks.

19 TL at TJ. No SP (Radipole Lane). Follow road round, ignore the left turn and cross over the A354.

20 TR no SP (Radipole Park Drive). Note that there is a cycleway on the right hand side of this road as it runs alongside the Lake Nature Reserve. ***36km (22.5 miles)***

21 TL at roundabout SP Station (Kings Street) and back to the Clock Tower and the end of the route. ***40km (25 miles)***

Route **14**

BLANDFORD FORUM AND CRANBORNE CHASE

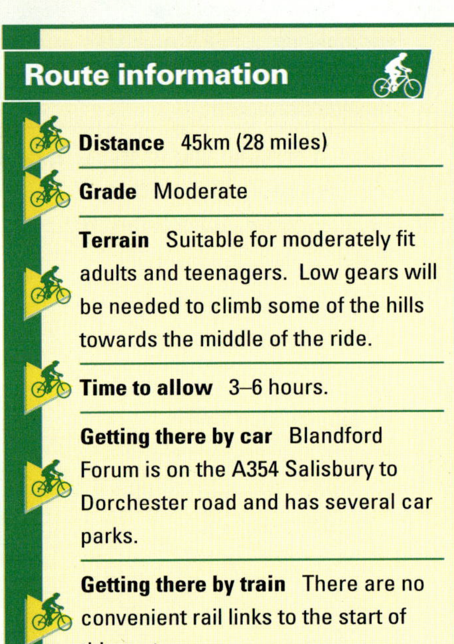

Route information

Distance 45km (28 miles)

Grade Moderate

Terrain Suitable for moderately fit adults and teenagers. Low gears will be needed to climb some of the hills towards the middle of the ride.

Time to allow 3–6 hours.

Getting there by car Blandford Forum is on the A354 Salisbury to Dorchester road and has several car parks.

Getting there by train There are no convenient rail links to the start of this route.

Starting in the Georgian market town of Blandford Forum on the River Stour, the route follows the river valley, before climbing to Tarrant Rushton Airfield with its World War II connections. Then down to Witchampton, with its 15th-century church and thatch and timber-framed cotttages. The ride then climbs once again, before heading for Cranborne Chase (King John's hunting grounds). After crossing the A354, the route climbs past the village of Farnham, into Tollard Royal and steeply on up, with extensive views of Ashcombe Bottom and the downland of Cranborne Chase. The route swings left, climbing to Ashmore, the highest village in Dorset, before plunging downhill into Washer's Pit. Then the last steep climb to the top of Fontmell Hill, before the descent to Blandford Forum, with extensive views of the Downs and Blackmoor Vale.

Places of interest along the route

A Royal Signals Museum, Blandford Forum

The museum tells the story of the Royal Corps of Signals and British military communications from the Crimean War to the present day. Take a driving licence or some similar form of identification containing your name, address and signature as you will need a security pass to visit the museum. Open all year (except ten days at Christmas), Monday-Friday 1000–1700; also weekends June to September 1000–1700. Charge.

B Tarrant Rushton Airfield

This airfield was the station for 298 and 644 squadrons and C glider squadron during World War II. The glider squadron had a very active role in the D Day landings in Normandy. Today on the site there is a memorial to those who were stationed on the airfield, and the wooden hangers remain standing. On the approach to the airfield are magnificent views across the Stour valley towards Blandford Forum.

C Larmer Tree, Victorian Pleasure Gardens, Tollard Royal

Situated off the cycle route, the gardens were created by General Pitt Rivers, a 19th-century archaeologist. Amongst the many features are buildings from northern India, a classical Roman temple and an open air museum. Tearoom. Open April to September, Thursdays, Sundays and public holidays 1100–1800; also mid July to August, Monday–Wednesday, 1100– 1800. Charge. Telephone (01725) 516228.

D Ashmore Village

The highest village in Dorset at 217m (700 feet). The village has a picturesque pond surrounded by fine flint stone thatched cottages. It was mentioned in the Domesday book of 1086 as Aisemare.

Food and drink

There are several restaurants, pubs and cafés in Blandford Forum.

Keynston Mill
Restaurant and fruit farm for morning coffees, light lunches and afternoon tea.

King John Inn, Tollard Royal
Real ales and bar meals.

NAAFI, Blandford Camp
Inside the museum.

Dorset countryside

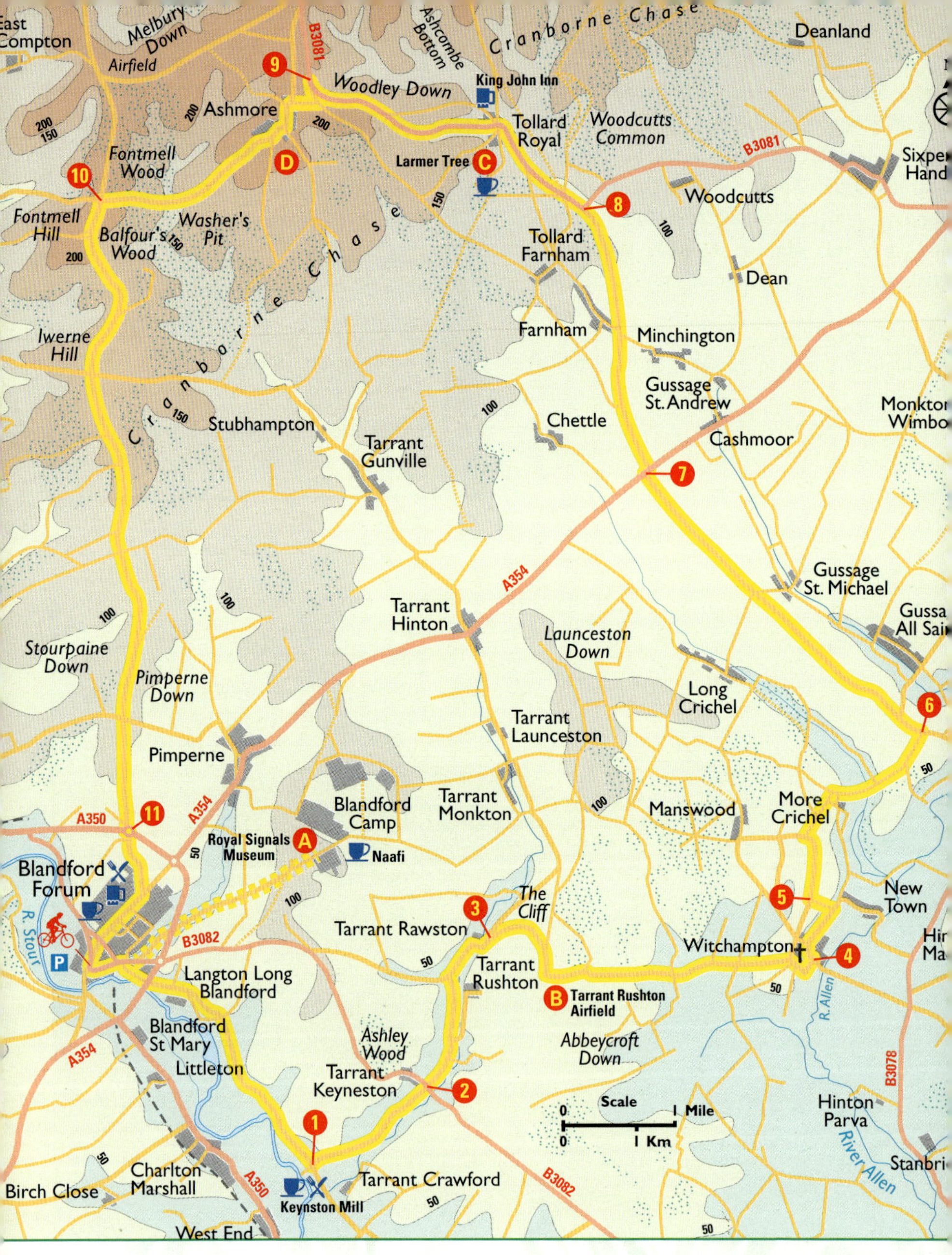
Cranborne Chase
Deanland
East Compton
Melbury Down
Airfield
Ashcombe Bottom
Woodley Down
King John Inn
Ashmore
Tollard Royal
Woodcutts Common
Fontmell Wood
Larmer Tree
Sixpenny Handley
Woodcutts
Fontmell Hill
Balfour's Wood
Washer's Pit
Tollard Farnham
Dean
Iwerne Hill
Farnham
Minchington
Gussage St. Andrew
Chettle
Cashmoor
Stubhampton
Tarrant Gunville
Gussage St. Michael
Tarrant Hinton
Launceston Down
Stourpaine Down
Pimperne Down
Long Crichel
Tarrant Launceston
Pimperne
Blandford Camp
Tarrant Monkton
Manswood
More Crichel
Royal Signals Museum
Naafi
Blandford Forum
R. Stour
The Cliff
New Town
Tarrant Rawston
Witchampton
Tarrant Rushton
Langton Long Blandford
Tarrant Rushton Airfield
R. Allen
Blandford St Mary
Ashley Wood
Abbeycroft Down
Littleton
Tarrant Keyneston
Scale
1 Mile
1 Km
Hinton Parva
River Allen
Charlton Marshall
Tarrant Crawford
Birch Close
Keynston Mill
West End
B3081
A354
A350
B3082
B3078

Route description 

Leave Blandford Forum via the B3082 (Langton Lane, off East Street/Wimborne Road), taking the path alongside the River Stour and under the A350 Blandford Bypass. Upon emerging on the other side turn right towards Langton Long. To visit the Royal Signals Museum, continue on B3082 and take next left, SP Blandford Camp.

1 TL, SP Tarrant Keyneston.

---

2 SO across B3082 (care needed), SP Tarrant Rushton.

---

3 TR up steep climb, The Cliff, to Tarrant Rushton Airfield and continue to Witchampton.

---

4 At TJ in Witchampton village centre, TL up hill and follow road round to the second left and up hill. ***12 km (7.5 miles)***

---

5 Arrive Rest and be Thankful seat where TR, SP More Crichel and Gussage All Saints. Follow road round to right and up the tree lined avenue.

---

6 TL along undulating road.

---

7 Arrive junction with A354. TR then immediately TL, SP Farnham and Tollard Royal. ***26km (16 miles)***

---

8 Bear left onto B3081 into Tollard Royal and start to climb up onto Cranborne Chase.

---

9 On the penultimate ridge of the climb turn sharp left, SP Ashmore. TR then TL at next junction into Ashmore village. The road drops steeply down from here into Washer's Pit and then climbs very steeply between Fontmell and Balfour's Wood.

---

10 TL, SP Blandford. ***34 km (21 miles)***

---

11 At roundabout junction with A350 Blandford ring road, carry SO, SP Industrial Estate, and follow SP to town centre and the finish of the route. ***45 km (28 miles)***

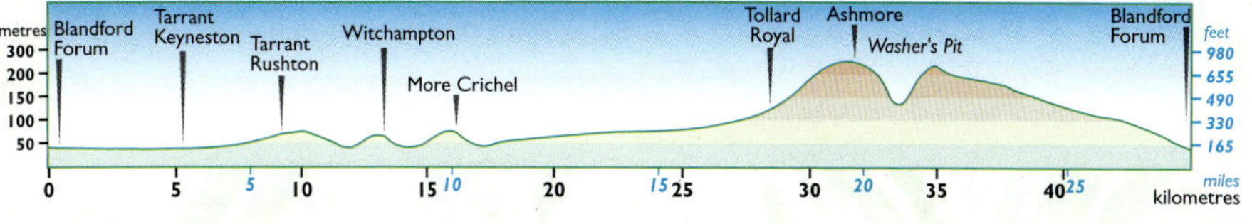

Route 15

CORFE CASTLE AND ISLE OF PURBECK

Route information

Distance 45.5km (28.5 miles)

Grade Moderate

Terrain Mostly country lanes, with some quiet B roads and two sections of bridleway. There are three short, but steep climbs on this route.

Time to allow 4 hours.

Getting there by car Wareham can be reached on the A35/A351 from Poole in the east and on the A352 from Dorchester in the west. There are several signposted car parks in the town but use the long-term car park in Streche Road, off West Street.

Getting there by train Wareham is on the main Waterloo to Weymouth line and has a frequent service. Telephone (0345) 484950 for information.

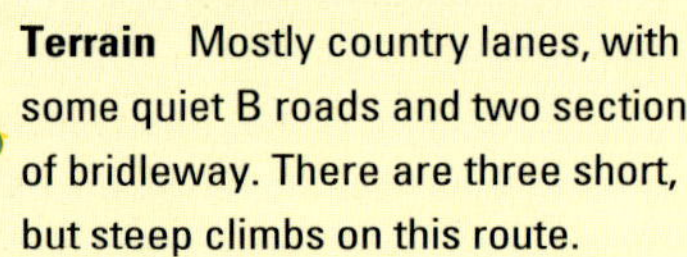

From Wareham across the causeway of the River Frome water meadow (which gives Purbeck its island character). The route then crosses the ridge of the Purbeck Hills and continues up onto the coastal escarpment. Only those who are very fit and with the lowest gears will attempt to ride the short, steep and rocky track to Smedmore Hill, but the views will take your breath away. The route heads east past the Purbeck stone quarries and then north, before turning to Corfe Castle along the route of an old tramway. The return to Wareham crosses Hartland Moor Nature Reserve.

Places of interest along the route

A Wareham

Wareham is designated an outstanding conservation area, contains over 200 listed buildings, and has a fascinating history reaching back to the Iron Age. **Wareham Museum**, East Street, tells the history of the town and has a section on T.E. Lawrence (Lawrence of Arabia). Open Easter to mid October, Monday–Saturday 1000–1700. Admission free. Telephone (01929) 553448.

B Blue Pool, Furzebrook

Once the site of a claypit, the pool is surrounded by 10ha (25 acres) of heather, gorse, pine trees and sandy paths. The blue colour of the water (particularly strong in cold weather) is caused by diffraction of light from particles of clay still suspended in the water. Tearoom, gift shop, museum and plant centre. Bicycles must be left at the entrance gate. Grounds open March to November, daily 0930–dusk. Tearoom, shops and museum open Easter to early October, daily 0930–1700. Charge. Telephone (01929) 551408.

C Kimmeridge

Kimmeridge is a picturesque village from where there is a toll road (free to cyclists) to Kimmeridge Bay, with its rocky shore and ledges and information kiosk. Access at all reasonable times. Free.

D Swyre Head

Swyre Head is absolutely the best place to view the sweep of the Dorset coastline, from St Aldhelm's Head in the east to the Isle of Portland in the west. This cliff ridge is a favourite for paragliding enthusiasts. Access at all reasonable times. Free.

E Stone Quarries

These quarries are where the Purbeck stone comes from. This soft limestone can be seen in many of the houses throughout the region and also in government buildings in London. Fossils are common in this stone and quarry owners can be approached for a souvenir, if you can carry the weight.

F Swanage Railway

This steam railway operates daily throughout the summer between Swanage and Corfe Castle. Bikes are carried with pleasure and you could use this trip to shorten your return journey. For fares and timetables telephone (01929) 424276.

G Corfe Castle

Impressive ruins of a once important stronghold, treasury and prison. The castle was destroyed by parliamentary forces in 1646. Events are held throughout the year. National Trust Property. Open March to November, daily 1000–1730; December to February, daily 1100–1530. Charge. Telephone (01929) 481294.

H World of Toys

Situated in the grounds of Arne House, this museum is based on a private collection of toys amassed over the past 25 years. Displays include boats, planes, cars, trains, steam engines, automated toys, teddy bears, dolls, dolls houses and musical boxes. Tearoom. Open April to June and September, Tuesday–Friday and Sunday 1330–1700; July and August, daily 1030–1730. Also open on Bank Holidays. Charge. Telephone (01929) 552018.

Food and drink

Wareham and Corfe Castle village have numerous pubs, cafés and tearooms. There are tearooms at the Blue Pool and the World of Toys Museum.

Scott Arms, Kingston
Overlooking Corfe Castle. Local beers, restaurant and bar meals. Garden.

Cowshed Tearooms, Langton Matravers
At Putlake Farm, on your right before you reach the A351, between directions 7 and 8.

Tearooms, Studland
On your right by the green.

Corfe Castle

Route description

From the car park take West Street and TR at the traffic lights into South Street. SO across South Bridge on B3075.

1 Cross roundabout with A351 (with care), SP Furzebrook.

2 Pass the Blue Pool on your left. Keep left. Climb zig zag of Ridgeway hill by the quarry. Excellent viewpoint at the top. Be careful of the narrow, steep descent. ***5km (3 miles***

---

3 SO at XR, SP Puddle Hill and Bradle.

---

4 To visit Kimmeridge village and the bay, TR at TJ. Otherwise, just before TJ look for steep, stony vehicle-wide bridleway on the left – take this and climb to Smedmore Hill.

9.5km (6 miles)

5 Follow bridleway along escarpment. There are some gates to negotiate on the way to Swyre Head.

6 Follow bridleway along the other side of Swyre Head, with Encombe House down to the right. There is one gate before meeting a tarmac road (the private driveway to Encombe), where TL and immediately TR to Kingston.

7 TR onto B3069, SP Swanage.

15km (9.5 miles)

8 TR onto A351 (with care), SP Swanage.

20km (12.5 miles)

9 TL into Washpond Lane (just before the Royal Oak). Continuing on the main road here takes you into the centre of Swanage. Follow the coast road and signs to Studland to rejoin route by going SO at direction 12.

10 TR, no SP. ***21.5km (13.5 miles)***

11 TL on corner, no SP. ***22.5km (14 miles)***

12 TL at TJ, no SP. ***23km (14.5 miles)***

13 Take RHF, SP Studland. Short climb to come before dropping down to Studland.

24km (15 miles)

14 Pass Knoll House Hotel on left, follow road downhill and continue up slight rise. As road curves right, TL onto bridleway (on left by the busstop), SP Greenlands Farm.

15 Pass Greenlands Farm on your right. Keep right along track and continue through gate, then keeping left with SP Goathorn Farm only on your right. Arrive tarmac road and TL.

30km (18.5 miles)

16 Tarmac road becomes unsurfaced and then meets XR with another tarmac road where TL, no SP. (These bridleways have been surfaced for oil-field traffic). ***32km (20 miles)***

17 TR and past Higher Bushey Farm.

33.5km (21 miles)

18 TL, no SP. ***35km (21.5 miles)***

19 TR onto B3351, SP Corfe Castle.

20 TL to visit the castle and village, then retrace and continue along A351 up the rise to roundabout.

21 At roundabout, TR off A351 and immediately TL (do not take oilfield road).

22 TR to visit the World of Toys Museum at Arne. Otherwise TL, no SP. ***41km (25.5 miles)***

23 TR at TJ, SP Wareham and retrace route to the car park and the end of the route.

45.5km (28.5 miles)

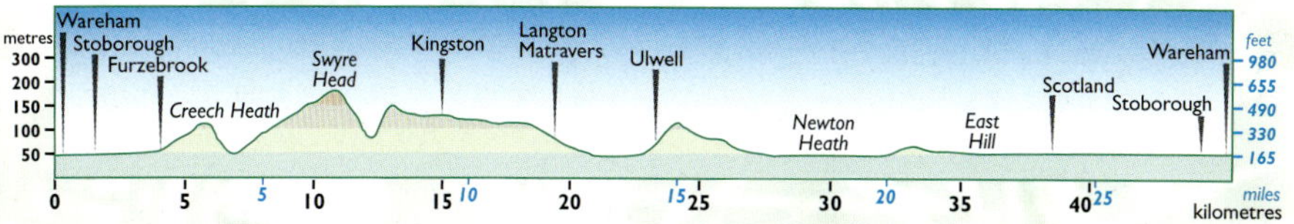

Route **16**

LYME REGIS AND MARSHWOOD VALE

Route information

Distance 56km (35 miles)

Grade Strenuous

Terrain Narrow, undulating unclassified minor roads and quiet B roads. Some difficult climbs.

Time to allow 5–7 hours.

Getting there by car Bridport is on the A35 Folkestone to Honiton road. There is a large car park in the centre of the town.

Getting there by train There are no convenient rail links to the start of this route.

Make no mistake, this is tough cycling country but, as always, the hills make the views worth the effort. The route starts at Bridport and then crosses the flatter lands of the lush Marshwood Vale, before heading to the coast. After climbing out of Lyme Regis, the route follows as flat a line as is possible along the Dorset and Devon border, around the edge of the Vale under Pilsdon Pen, Dorset's highest point. Then, through the village of Broadwindsor and on to the small town of Beaminster. The terrain becomes easier as you return to Bridport.

Places of interest along the route

A Lyme Regis

It is worth parking the bike and taking a walk around Lyme Regis, a settlement since at least the 8th century. The Cobb, a breakwater first constructed during the 13th century, more recently featured in the film *The French Lieutenant's Woman*. The town is famous for fossils and **Dinosaurland Fossil World** contains a fossil shop, Jurassic exhibition and Time Gallery. Open all year, daily 1000–1700. Charge for exhibition and gallery. Telephone (01297) 443541. **Lyme Regis Marine Aquarium and Cobb History** is housed in the historic Cobb Warehouse. There are tanks of Lyme Bay fish, old fishing gear, marine bygone sand wreckage. An historic photograph collection includes photos of the filming of *The French Lieutenant's Woman*. Open Easter to October, daily 1000–1700. Charge. Telephone (01297) 443678. The **Lyme Regis Philpot Museum** contains displays on local geology and history. Open April to October, weekends and school half-terms in winter, Monday–Saturday 1000–1700, Sunday 1000–1200 and 1400–1700. Charge.

B Pilsdon Pen

Dorset's highest point at 277m (909 feet). The road does not go over the top but it is accessible by a footpath from the road.

C Horn Park Gardens

A large garden with magnificent views to the sea. Features rock gardens, terraces and herbaceous borders, woodland garden and wild flower meadow. Open April to October Tuesday, Wednesday and Sunday 1400–1800 Charge. Telephone (01308) 862212.

Food and drink 

Lyme Regis and Bridport have many cafés and restaurants.

Five Bells Inn, Whitchurch Canonicorum
Real ales.

Piggy Bank Café, Charmouth
Morning coffee, lunches and cream teas.

Pickwicks Inn, Beaminster
Café/bar with excellent meals.

Hare and Hounds, Waytown
Grills and snacks.

D Parnham House
A large tudor house completely restored by John Makepiece, the furniture designer. The house is a workshop for master craftsmen in wood and is used to display exquisite commissioned pieces prior to delivery. Shop, gardens, teashop and specially-designed children's play area. Open Easter to October, Tuesday–Thursday and Sunday 1000–1700. Charge. Telephone (01308) 862204.

Route description 

TL on leaving the car park, heading west out of Bridport.

1 At western end TR on the roundabout, SP Salwayash and Broadwindsor.

2 TL, SP Broadoak, onto a very narrow lane and enter the Marshwood Vale.

Lyme Regis

3 Arrive Shave Cross and TL by Shave Cross Inn, SP Whitchurch and Charmouth.

8km (5 miles)

4 In Whitchurch Canonicorum, TR by Five Bells Inn, SP Wootton Fitzpaine. ***11km (7 miles)***

5 SO, SP Charmouth.

6 TR, after National School, SP Wootton Fitzpaine.

7 Keep left, SP Wootton Fitzpaine.

14.5km (9 miles)

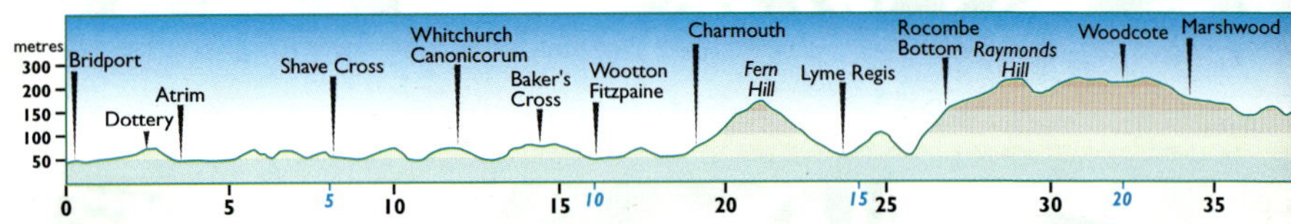

8 Keep left, SP Charmouth.

9 Keep left, SP Charmouth.

15.5km (9.5 miles)

10 TR, SP Lyme Regis, and cycle up Charmouth main street.

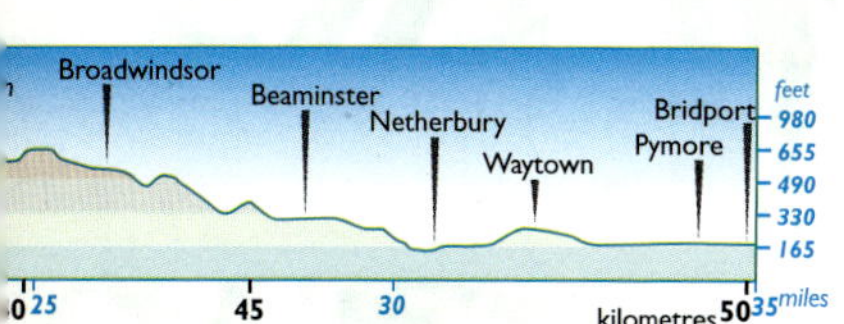

11 TL at first exit on roundabout, SP Lyme Regis. This road continues uphill for a little longer and then drops steeply down into Lyme (Dragon's Hill). In the town at the bottom the road narrows and there is a short traffic light controlled section just before reaching the sea. Continue on round and up through the town.

12 RHF (after most of the shopping area), SP Axminster. ***22.5km (14 miles)***

13 TR into minor road (downhill at first), SP Rocombe Half and Rhode Hill. Continue uphill on either of the two parallel roads to Red Cross XR – tough gradient.

24km (15 miles)

14 SO at Red Cross XR at top of hill, crossing A35 with care. ***27km (17 miles)***

15 TR, SP Marshwood. Continue on B3165.

16 TR, SP Broadwindsor, climbing gently past the foot of Pilsdon Pen, with views to the right over the whole of Marshwood Vale.

35km (21.5 miles)

17 TR and follow one-way system through Broadwindsor, SP Beaminster. Just beyond the village there is a sharp hill with an equally sharp descent. ***41.5km (26 miles)***

18 To visit Horn Park Gardens, TL onto A3066, SP Crewkerne. Otherwise, TR at TJ, SP Bridport and Town Centre. Parnham House is on the right on leaving the town.

45.5km (28.5 miles)

19 TR, SP Netherbury.

20 Bear right, SP Bowood and Broadwindsor. ***48km (30 miles)***

21 TL, SP Waytown and Bridport.

22 TL at TJ, SP Bridport. ***53.5km (33 miles)***

23 TR, SP Pymore and Bridport.

24 TR in Bridport to join main street and finish the route. ***56km (35 miles)***

Route 17

ISLE OF WIGHT – WESTERN LOOP

Route information

Distance 57.5km (35.5 miles)

Grade Moderate – inexperienced or weaker cyclists may need to walk one or two short hills.

Terrain For the most part, the route avoids main roads. There are only two significant climbs, one from Calbourne over Brighstone Down (compensated by a long run down into Brighstone), and the other a climb out of Carisbrooke on the B3401. The path south from Yarmouth is well maintained and the optional piece of track after Yafford is suitable for all cycles.

Time to allow 3½–4 hours.

Getting there by car Lymington is on the A337 and there is a car park at the ferry terminal. There are regular passenger and car ferry sailing between Lymington and Yarmouth. Both services carry bicycles free of charge. Telephone (0990) 827744 for information on fares and sailing times.

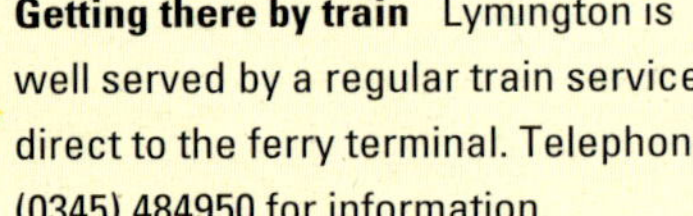

Getting there by train Lymington is well served by a regular train service direct to the ferry terminal. Telephone (0345) 484950 for information.

Places of interest along the route

A Yarmouth Castle, Yarmouth

Yarmouth Castle is one of Henry VIII's coastal defences and was completed in 1547. Climb the battlements for superb views over the Solent. Exhibition of local paintings and photographs of old Yarmouth. Open March to October, daily 1000–1300 and 1400–1800 (or dusk if earlier). Charge. Telephone (01983) 760678.

B Chessell Pottery, Chessell

Visitors can watch the complete production of exquisite porcelain, from the preparation of the porcelain clay through to decorating and firing the finished articles. Technical and historical exhibition. Studios open all year, Monday–Saturday 0900–1700. Showroom and coffee shop open all year, Monday–Saturday 0900–1730. Showroom also open Easter to Christmas, Sunday 1000–1700. Nominal charge. Telephone (01983) 531248.

C Calbourne Water Mill and Rural Museum

A 17th-century water mill, still operating and producing flour, set in beautifully kept grounds (good place for a picnic). Nostalgia museum and old vehicles, ducks, peacocks and doves. Café and gift shop. Open Easter to October, daily 1000–1730. Charge. Telephone (01983) 531227.

D Winkle Street

A much-photographed beauty spot.

E Yafford Mill and Farm Park, Shorwell

Working water mill and agricultural museum set in 14.5ha (36 acres) of woodland and water-

Food and drink 

Refreshments are available on the ferry. Yarmouth has numerous shops, cafés and pubs. The tearoom at Clamerkin is separate from the Farm Park. Brighstone has a café and convenience stores and you will find pubs and convenience stores in Carisbrooke and a post office/store in Shalfleet.

Sun, Calbourne
Local ales and bar snacks.

New Inn, Shalfleet
Bar snacks available.

Three Bishops, Brighstone
Local ales and bar food.

Coopers Inn, Brighstone
Pub and tearoom .

park. Farm animals (including many rare breeds), birds and waterfowl, and Sophie, a grey seal. Nature trail alongside mill stream. Children's playground, restaurant and gift shop. Open all year, daily 1000–1800 (dusk if earlier). Charge. Telephone (01983) 740610 (mill); (01983) 741125 (museum).

F Carisbrooke Castle
A fortress and prison with royal connections dating from the early 13th century. Donkey centre, World War I Memorial Chapel and museum. Gift shop. Picnic in the grounds or visit the restaurant. Self-guided audio tour and personal guides. Open March to October, daily 1000–1800 (or dusk if earlier). Charge. Telephone English Heritage on 0171 973 3434 for further information.

G Clamerkin Farm Park, near Newtown
Situated on the banks of the Newtown Estuary and covering 12ha (30 acres). Working farm with opportunities to meet the animals face to face, feed and touch them. Museum of Island Brick-making, nature trail and picnic area. Gift shop. Tearoom. Open Easter to October, daily 1030–1730. Charge. Telephone (01983) 531396.

Route description 

Leave the ferry and TR at roundabout onto A3054, SP Newport and Ryde. Take the second right into Victoria Road. TR onto the Bridleway at the end of Victoria Road.

1 TL onto road (follow cycleway sign). Then at TJ TL onto B3399, SP Newport.

3km (2 miles)

Calbourne Water Mill

2 At XR SO onto the B3401. Continue, passing Calbourne Mill at 10.5km (6.5 miles). After Calbourne Mill, bear right towards Calbourne.

3 Arrive Calbourne (11.5km/7 miles). At XR TR, SP Brighstone and Winkle Street. Climb to Brighstone Down and descend into Brighstone.

4 At TJ with B3399, TL.

5 Continue past Brighstone church and TR into Broad Lane, following cycleway sign.

16.5km (10.5 miles)

6 At TJ TL, SP Atherfield and Yafford.

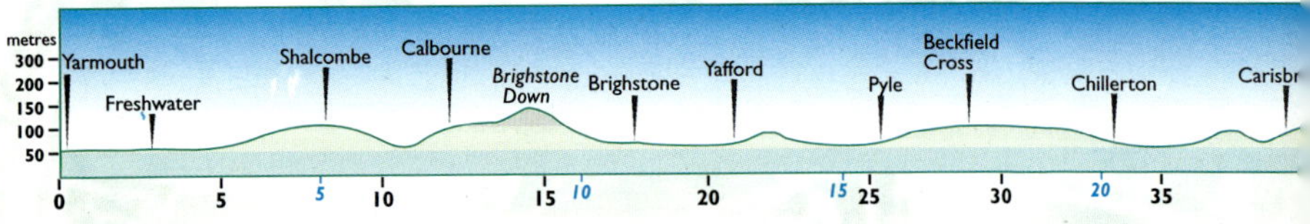

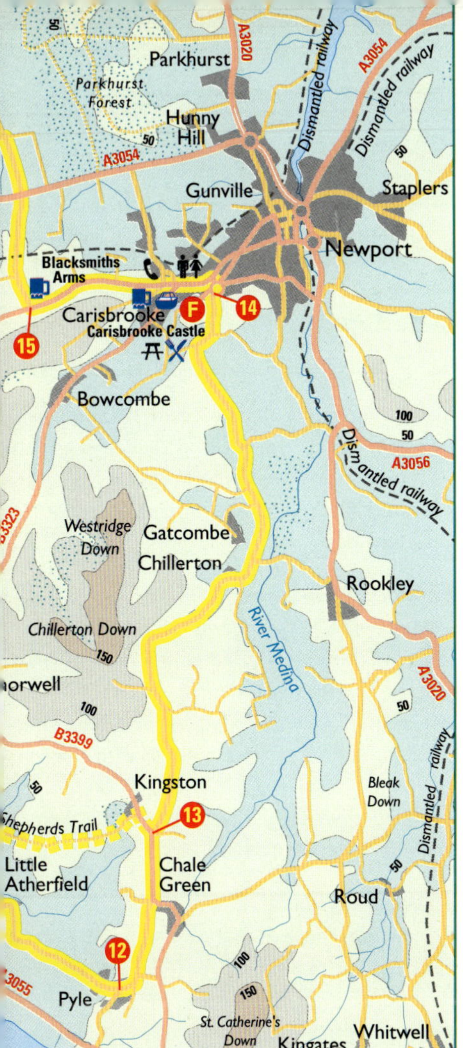

7 TL, SP Yafford. ***18.5km (11.5 miles)***

8 TR, SP Yafford, and pass Yafford Mill. **20km (12.5 miles)**

9 At TJ TR and then TL, SP Atherfield and Chale (follow cycleway sign).

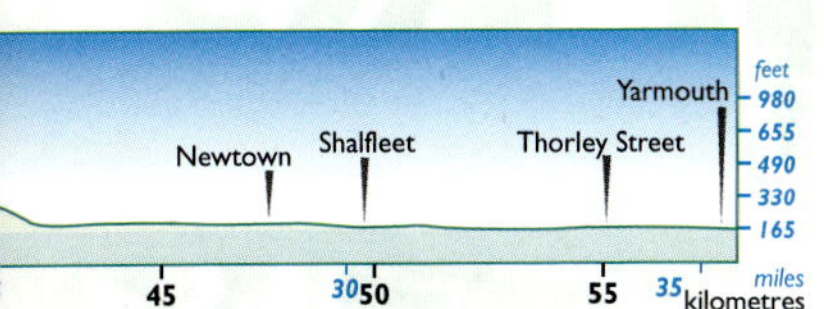

10 TR at TJ, SP Atherfield.

11 For optional route along bridleway, TL onto Shepherds Trail, SP Kingston (22.5km/14 miles). At TJ with B3399, TR and rejoin route at direction 13 and TL, SP Chillerton. Otherwise, continue route by bearing left at next junction.

12 At junction (25.5km/16 miles), SO along Chale Lane (ignore cycleway sign), then at TJ TL, SP Shorwell, Brighstone and Newport.

13 SO, SP Chillerton. Continue through and beyond village to Carisbrooke. ***27.5km (17 miles)***

14 In Carisbrooke, SO at Cedar Hill roundabout. At TJ TL into Carisbrooke High Street. At mini roundabout, SO, SP Calbourne.

15 TR beside Blacksmiths Arms, no SP (40.5km/25 miles). Continue to XR with A3054 where SO, SP Thorness and Cowes. Then TL, SP Porchfield and Newtown.

16 TL at TJ , SP Shalfleet.

17 TR at XR, SP Newtown (follow cycleway sign). ***45km (28 miles)***

18 TR at TJ. Then TR at TJ with A3054, SP Shalfleet and Yarmouth (ignore cycleway sign). Note there are traffic signals into Shalfleet.

19 TL before church (into one way street). ***49km (30.5 miles)***

20 TL at TJ, no SP, and TL at next TJ, no SP, onto B3401.

21 TR (as B3401 bends left) into Wellow Top Road, SP Wellow and Yarmouth. ***51.5km (32 miles)***

22 TL at TJ onto B3401 (follow cycleway sign). Keep on the B3401 and and return to Yarmouth and the ferry terminal.

Route **18**

DORCHESTER AND WHITE HORSE HILL

Route information

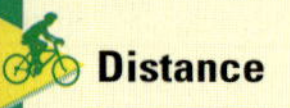

Distance 58km (36 miles)

Grade Strenuous

Terrain Mostly off-road, using tracks and high ridgeways. There are few refreshment stops.

Time to allow 4–7 hours.

Getting there by car Dorchester is on the A35 Folkestone to Honiton road. Car parking is available at the Top o' Town opposite Hardy's Statue.

Getting there by train Dorchester is on the Waterloo to Weymouth main line and has a frequent service. It is also on a line that intersects with Yeovil Junction. Telephone (0345) 484950 for information.

From Dorchester, skirting Maiden Castle, the route climbs to Hardy's Monument using large sections of bridleway. Then follows a classic ridgeway route, travelling east along the South West Coast Path and White Horse Hill, before returning to Dorchester by an interesting series of roads and bridleways. Although sixty per cent of the route is off-road, the tracks are easily ridden and a mountain bike is not essential.

Places of interest along the route

A Dorchester

Dorchester is the County Town of Dorset and has many old streets and buildings. It is well known as the writer Thomas Hardy's Casterbridge. See route 3 for places of interest in Dorchester.

B Hardy's Monument

Monument to Admiral Hardy, of 'Kiss me Hardy' fame, as Nelson lay dying on the deck of *HMS Victory*. This monument commands spectacular 360 degree panoramic views and has been restored so that visitors can climb to the top. National Trust Property. Open March to September, weekends only 1100–1700. Charge. Telephone (01985) 843600.

C White Horse Hill

So called because of the giant figure on horse-back cut out of the turf, covering almost 0.5ha (1 acre). The figure is George III, on his horse, riding away from Weymouth.

D Llewelyn Powys Monument

Llewelyn Powys was one of a remarkable trio of literary brothers from Dorchester. He was extremely fond of walking and this monument stands in his memory.

E Mill House Cider and Clock Museum

An exhibition of early cider equipment with a video of cider presses in use. Also a collection of Longcase and Turret clocks. Café. Open April to October, daily 1000–1700; November to March, Tuesday–Sunday 1000-1600. Telephone (01305) 852220.

Food and drink

Dorchester

There are many cafés, restaurants and hotels of all standards in Dorchester but for basic fare try the A35 Café (well known by all local club cyclists) in the car park at Top o' Town, at the start and finish of this route.

Brewers Arms, Martinstown

Local ales and bar meals.

Sailors Return, East Chaldon

Local ales and bar meals.

Wise Man Inn, West Stafford

Local ales and bar meals.

Route description

Leave Dorchester's Top o' Town car park by the Bridport Road exit and TR to travel west. At traffic lights TL then TR into Damers Road. TL into Maud Road.

1 TR into Maiden Castle Road, crossing the bypass via the bridge.

2 TR onto bridleway, SP Martinstown. Good views of Maiden Castle, the largest hillfort in Europe.

3 At Clandon Farm follow tarmac drive through farmyard then TL through gate.

4 Cross road to path skirting football field, SP Martinstown.

5 TL onto tarmac drive. TR onto B3159. Continue through the village of Martinstown.

White Horse Hill

6 At Lower Rew, TL onto bridleway to South Rew.

7 TR onto road and continue up to Hardy's Monument. ***11 km (7 miles)***

8 TL onto bridleway just before the monument, where the road dips down, SP Inland Route, Corton Hill. The route now follows the South West Coast Path and passes numerous tumuli.

9 Follow line of tumuli and continue to A354.

10 Cross A354 (with care – fast traffic, especially from the right).

11 As the road forks left take RHF onto chalk track. There is often a gypsy encampment along here.

12 TR, SP Inland Coast Path, Osmington. There are fine views of Weymouth Bay and Portland from here.

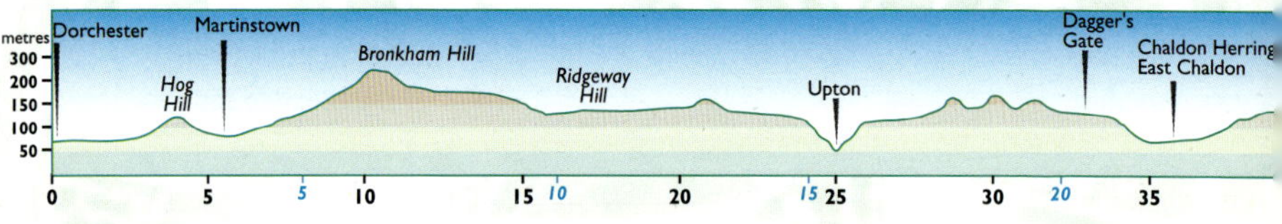

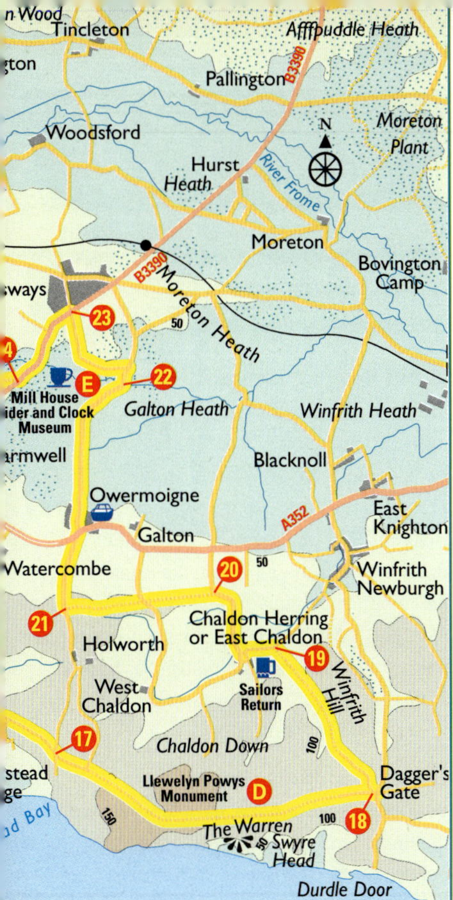

13 TL, SP Poxwell. Walk over crest of hill to view King George III on his White Horse riding away from Weymouth.

14 SO at XR of tracks, SP Holworth.

15 TR onto A353 (with care – watch out for speeding vehicles). ***26km (16 miles)***

16 Sharp TL, SP Ringstead. Keep on road, do not go down to Ringstead through toll gate.

17 Follow bridleway, SP West Lulworth, passing the monument to Llewelyn Powys. Great views of the coastline.

18 Sharp TL on bridleway at Daggers Gate. SP East Chaldon. ***34km (21 miles)***

19 TL onto road and TR at village green to pass the Sailors Return pub.

20 At top of hill, TL onto bridleway, SP White Horse Hill.

21 TR onto road to Owermoigne. Cross A352 and pass village shop.

22 Pass Mill House Cider and Clock Museum. TL onto bridleway, SP Dick o' the Banks. ***44km (27.5 miles)***

23 TL onto B3390. Pass Warmwell Leisure Centre.

24 TR onto bridleway over heathland.

25 TR onto tarmac track through watercress works and continue up bridleway to the left.

26 Skirt quarry by turning left, right and left by pylon.

27 Through gate, then left up shallow valley past Bottom Heath Barn.

28 TL then left and right onto concrete track.

29 TR onto road, then TL onto bridleway by lodge house.

30 TR to Sixpenny Gate and over railway bridge to West Stafford. TL past the Wise Man Inn (seats outside are recommended). ***53km (33 miles)***

31 TR onto bridleway. Continue past the municipal tip and sewage works for the run back in to Dorchester.

32 Continue up Fordington High Street and then Dorchester High Street to Top o' Town car park and the finish of the route. ***58km (36 miles)***

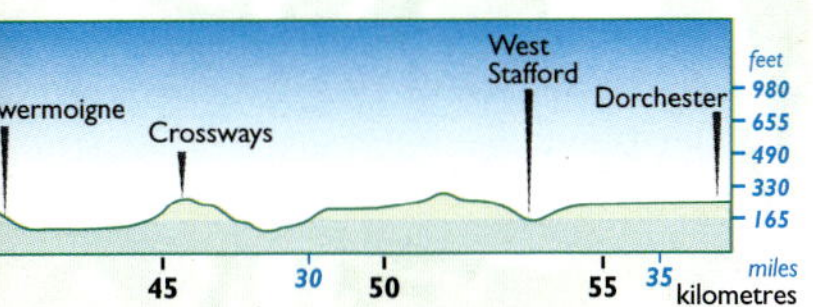

Route 19

HAMBLEDON AND THE FOREST OF BERE

Route information

Distance 68km (42 miles)

Grade Moderate

Terrain Mostly on unclassified roads. Note that the B2177 can be busy. The final short climb to Catherington and the one towards Butser Hill may prove difficult for less experienced cyclists on bikes without low gears. The length of optional track after Butser Hill is suitable for touring cycles and hybrids.

Time to allow 3½ hours

Getting there by car Wickham lies at the junction of the A32 (Alton to Fareham road) and the A334 (from Southampton). Parking in the centre of Wickham is time restricted, but there is a free car park signposted from the town centre.

Getting there by train There are no convenient rail links to the start of this route.

From Wickham south to Fort Nelson, overlooking Porstmouth and the Solent from Portsdown Hill. Then, northeast through country villages, before rounding Butser Hill and returning through the Hampshire countryside to Wickham.

Places of interest along the route

A Fort Nelson, Portsdown Hill

Fort Nelson was built in the 1860s as part of Lord Palmerston's defences to protect Portsmouth from a French invasion. The fort now houses the Royal Armouries Artillery Museum. The museum itself contains artillery of all ages from all over the world, from a medieval Turkish gun through to sections of the infamous Iraqi super-gun. Explore the tunnels, ammunition stores and mortar batteries, and climb the ramparts. Close to the fort is a monument to Lord Nelson.

B Old Idsworth Church,

A curiosity – an original, early church, with wall paintings. Associations with 1066, King Harold and the Godwin family.

C Cricket Memorial, Bat and Ball Pub

The memorial commemorates the birth of cricket and the time when the men of Hambledon played and defeated an all-England team.

Route description

Leave the centre of Wickham in an easterly direction. Cross the A32 and join the B2177, SP Southwick and Boarhunt. Continue towards Boarhunt.

1 TR at XR, SP South Boarhunt and Fareham. TL, SP Southwick (5km/3 miles), then TR SP Ashley Down and Portchester. Take LHF, SP Portchester (single track road) to Nelson's Monument.

Food and drink 

There are severel cafés in Wickham. The garden centre at Horndean has a tearoom. All major villages and towns on the route are well served by pubs and, in addition to the centres at Wickham, Denmead and Horndean, there are general stores at Southwick, Clanfield and Buriton.

Forest of Bere, Denmead
Passed early on in the route. Bar lunches.

Bird in Hand, Lovedean
Bar snacks available.

Master Robert, Buriton
Meals and snacks served.

Rising Sun, Clanfield
Locals pub. Bar snacks available.

Bat and Ball, Hambledon
Much cricketing memorabilia. Open fires. Bar snacks and restaurant.

Lotts Tearoom, Hambledon
Tea, coffee and snacks. Closes around 1615.

Old Idsworth Church

2 TR at XR to visit Fort Nelson. To continue route TL. Continue to XR where TL, no SP, and keep right to Southwick.

3 At roundabout with B2177, SO, SP Southwick (10.5km/6.5 miles). TR past church, SP Denmead. Continue to roundabout where SO, SP Denmead. Then TR at TJ, SP Waterlooville.

4 TL, SP Anmore and Catherington, past Forest of Bere pub. Continue following signs to Catherington.

5 TR about 1km (0.6 mile) after Bird in Hand pub.

6 TR at TJ then TL, no SP, into Five Heads Road. ***21.5km (13.5 miles)***

7 TL at TJ and cycle over A3 motorway. TR at roundabout, SP Rowlands Castle. TL, SP Rowlands Castle (garden centre and tearoom opposite) and follow signs to Rowlands Castle.

24km (15 miles)

8 Arrive Rowlands Castle. TR at TJ for teashops and pubs, otherwise TL at TJ, under railway bridge. Continue through Finchdean and past Old Idsworth Church at 32km/20 miles.

9 TL, SP Petersfield, over railway, then immediately TR, no SP, and continue to Buriton.

33.5km (21 miles)

10 TL at XR opposite Master Robert pub. SO at roundabout, SP East Meon. Cross A3 and continue towards East Meon.

11 TL into Harvesting Lane (45km/28 miles) and continue past Butser Hill.

12 TL at TJ for views over Meon Valley and Isle of Wight from Butser Hill. To continue route, TR at TJ, no SP.

13 For optional route, TR onto track (start of which is tarmacked).

a TL, SP Clanfield and rejoin route at direction 14.

Otherwise, SO to Clanfield (as road bears left).

14 Take road opposite Rising Sun pub, towards Hambledon. Then TR, SP Hambledon. SO at XR, SP Hambledon, passing cricket memorial and Bat and Ball pub on right. Continue to Hambledon.

15 Cycle through Hambledon. TL onto B2150 (Denmead road). TR, no SP, at Lotts Tearoom.

16 TL at XR, SP Southwick and Fareham.

59km (36.5 miles)

17 TR at TJ, no SP. Then TR at TJ.

18 TL at XR, SP Hundred Acres and Wickham.

19 TR at TJ onto B2177, SP Wickham, and return to Wickham to complete the route.

68km (42 miles)

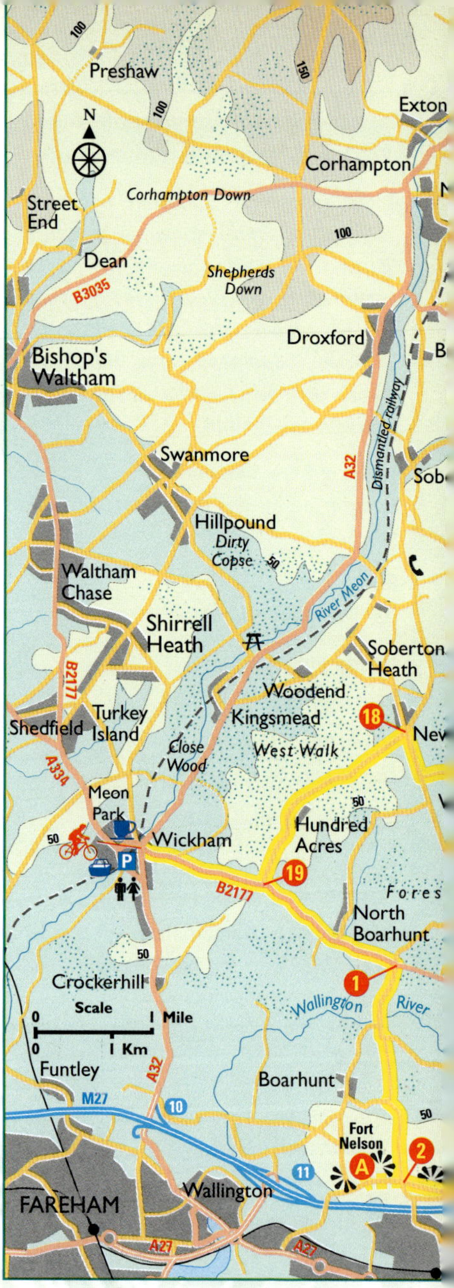

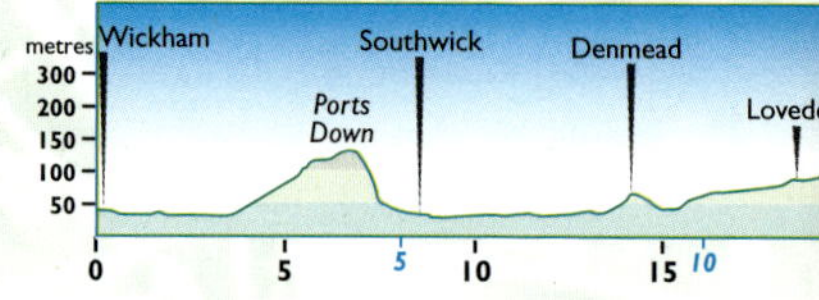

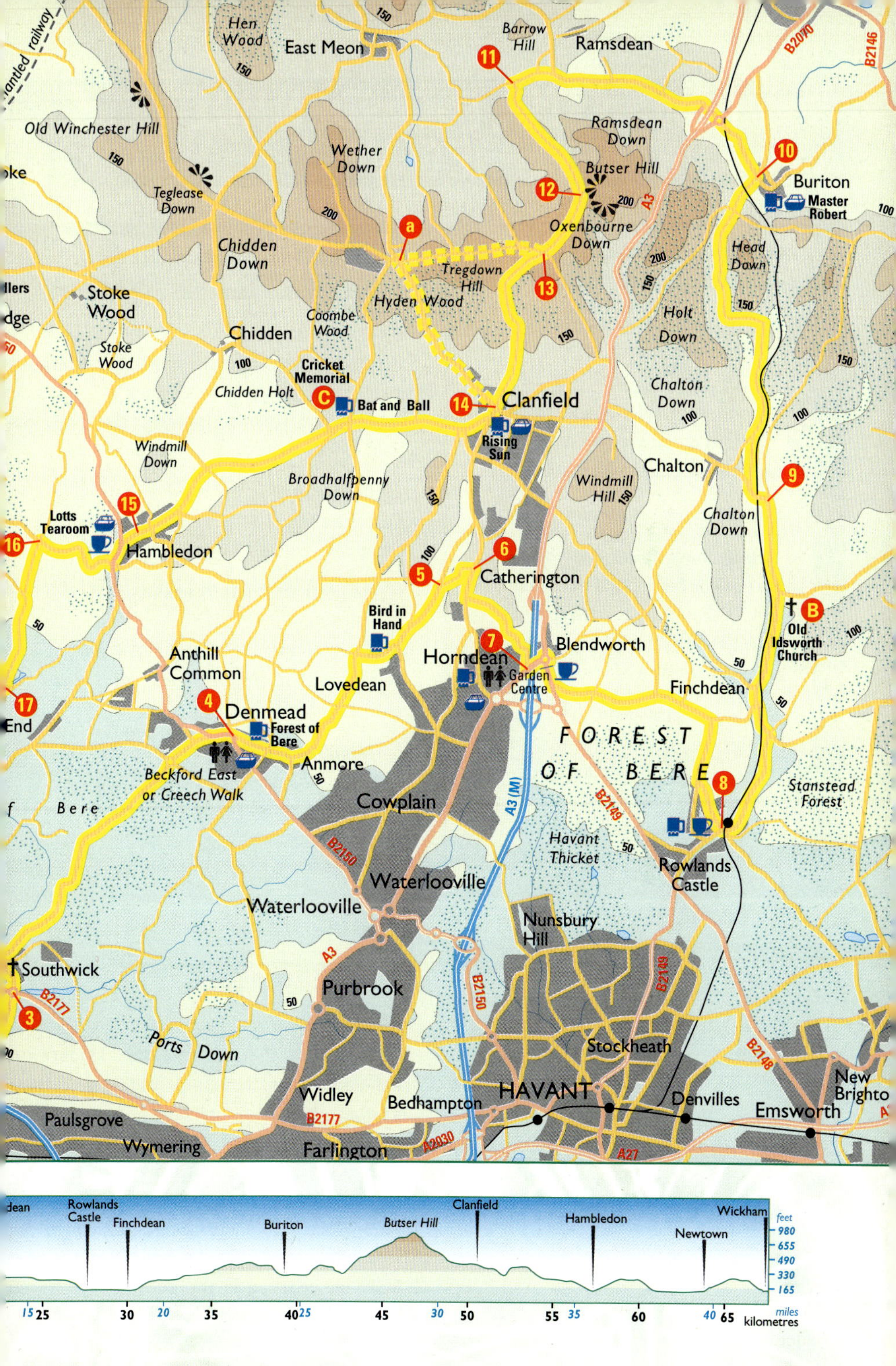

Hen Wood
East Meon
Barrow Hill
Ramsdean
Old Winchester Hill
Ramsdean Down
Wether Down
Butser Hill
Buriton
Master Robert
Teglease Down
Oxenbourne Down
Chidden Down
Tregdown Hill
Head Down
Stoke Wood
Hyden Wood
Holt Down
Chidden
Coombe Wood
Stoke Wood
Cricket Memorial
Chidden Holt
Bat and Ball
Clanfield
Chalton Down
Rising Sun
Windmill Down
Chalton
Broadhalfpenny Down
Windmill Hill
Lotts Tearoom
Chalton Down
Hambledon
Catherington
Bird in Hand
Old Idsworth Church
Anthill Common
Horndean
Blendworth
Garden Centre
Finchdean
Lovedean
Denmead
Forest of Bere
FOREST OF BERE
Anmore
Beckford East or Creech Walk
Stanstead Forest
Bere
Cowplain
Havant Thicket
Rowlands Castle
Waterlooville
Waterlooville
Nunsbury Hill
Southwick
Purbrook
Ports Down
Stockheath
Widley
Bedhampton
HAVANT
Denvilles
New Brighton
Emsworth
Paulsgrove
Wymering
Farlington
B2070
B2146
A3
A3(M)
B2149
B2150
B2177
B2148
A2030
A27
Rowlands Castle
Finchdean
Buriton
Butser Hill
Clanfield
Hambledon
Newtown
Wickham
feet
980
655
490
330
165
miles
kilometres

Route **20**

DORCHESTER, EGGARDON HILL AND THE CERNE GIANT

Route information

Distance 70km (43.5 miles)

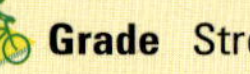

Grade Strenuous

Terrain High ridge roads, steep climbs and narrow country lanes. A reasonably quiet main road to finish.

Time to allow 4–7 hours.

Getting there by car Dorchester is on the A35 Folkestone to Honiton road. Car parking is available in Dorchester at the Top o' Town, opposite Hardy's Statue.

Getting there by train Dorchester is on the Waterloo to Weymouth main line and has a frequent service. There is also a rail link with Yeovil Junction. Telephone (0345) 484950 for information.

Out of Dorchester along a Roman road before climbing gradually up to Eggardon Hill. The route crosses the ridges of Dorset's downland along quiet country lanes, across the ridge of Toller Down and Batcombe Hill. You then head south along the Cerne Valley for a quick look at the Cerne Giant, before returning to Dorchester. Lots of Dorset's highest spots and plenty of climbs, but the views make it all worthwhile.

Places of interest along the route

A Dorchester

Dorchester is the County Town of Dorset and has many old streets and buildings. It is well known as the writer Thomas Hardy's Casterbridge. See Route 3 for places of interest in Dorchester.

B Eggardon Hill

Site of an Iron Age fort and worth the climb for tremendous views. Access at all times.

C Rampisham Radio Transmitter, Rampisham Hill

A major short wave transmitting station operated by the BBC World Service. The masts are visible for miles.

D Minterne Gardens, Minterne Magna

The gardens of Minterne Magna House comprise a valley landscaped during the 18th century: woodland garden with rare trees; rhododendrons and magnolias; lakes, cascades and streams. Spring bulbs and brilliant colours in the autumn. Quiet and informal. Open March to November, daily 1000–1900. Charge. Telephone (01300) 341370.

E Cerne Giant

The infamous 55m (180 feet) high landmark of the giant is a male nude carved into the chalk. Known locally as 'his mightiness', the giant is of ancient pagan origin and is thought to have been a fertility symbol. There was an old belief that a living giant who ate human flesh and terrorised the neighbourhood was captured and killed here, and that the outline of his huge body was carved in the chalk of the hillside where he lay.

Food and drink 

There are many cafés, restaurants and hotels of all standards in Dorchester. For basic fare (and known by all local club cyclists), the A35 Café in the car park at Top o' Town is highly recommended. Cerne Abbas has a variety of pubs, cafés and shops.

The Crown, Uploders
Local ales and bar snacks.

Acorn Inn, Evershot
Local ales and bar meals.

Smiths Arms, Godmanstone
England's smallest pub. Beer and bar snacks.

Route description 

Leave Dorchester's Top o' Town car park by the Bridport Road exit and immediately TR by the Military Museum. Continue along this undulating road, passing Poundbury Hillfort and making a fast descent over the Dorchester bypass. Note the remains of the Roman Aqueduct following the contours. Descend into Bradford Peverell and continue to Quatre Bras.

1 TL at Quatre Bras and continue towards Knowle Hill.

2 TR at XR at bottom of the hill, SP Compton Valence and ride to Eggardon Hill.

19km (12 miles)

3 TL (sharply), SP Askerswell. There is a superb view of Marshwood Vale to the right. A long fast descent passes the Spyway Inn, a pub with a view.

Cerne Giant

4 TR and then TL through the picturesque villages of Uploders (past the Crown Inn) and Loders. Continue under disused railway bridge.

26km (16 miles)

5 TR by telephone box, LHF over XR (all SP West Milton). Here the route passes through some delightful rural scenery.

6 TL, SP Bradpole.

7 TR, follow SP to Poorton.

8 Continue through Poorton and TR, SP Toller Porcorum. Then tackle the long but scenic climb to Mount Pleasant.

9 SO at XR, down the hill and SO at XR. Climb again up to the Rampisham radio masts.

10 SO at A356, towards Rampisham and Evershot.

44km (27.5 miles)

11 TR, SP Holywell. (The Acorn Inn and shops are on the left back into the village.)

12 SO at A37 (with great care). Climb the hill. Note the ancient Cross and Hand stone on the left. Pass the Gore Hill picnic site with commanding views across the Blackmoor Vale.

13 TR onto A352 (54km/33.5 miles). Although this is a main road and single file riding is recommended, traffic is not generally heavy. Continue to Cerne Abbas, passing Minterne Gardens on the left.

14 LHF into Cerne Abbas, with the vantage point to view the giant on the left.

15 TR and then TL to rejoin the A352. Continue on A352 through Godmanstone.

16 After the 30mph signs in Charminster, TL over the footbridge.

17 TL and up the hill, then round to the right and SO at the XR.

18 TR and cycle downhill, SP Dorchester.

19 In Dorchester, TL and climb the hill with the wall and grassy bank on your left. At the top of the hill, by Hardy's Statue, TR into Top o' Town car park to finish the route.

70km (43.5 miles)

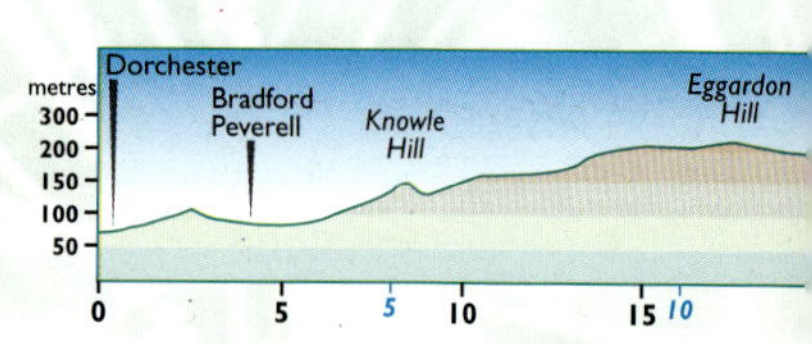

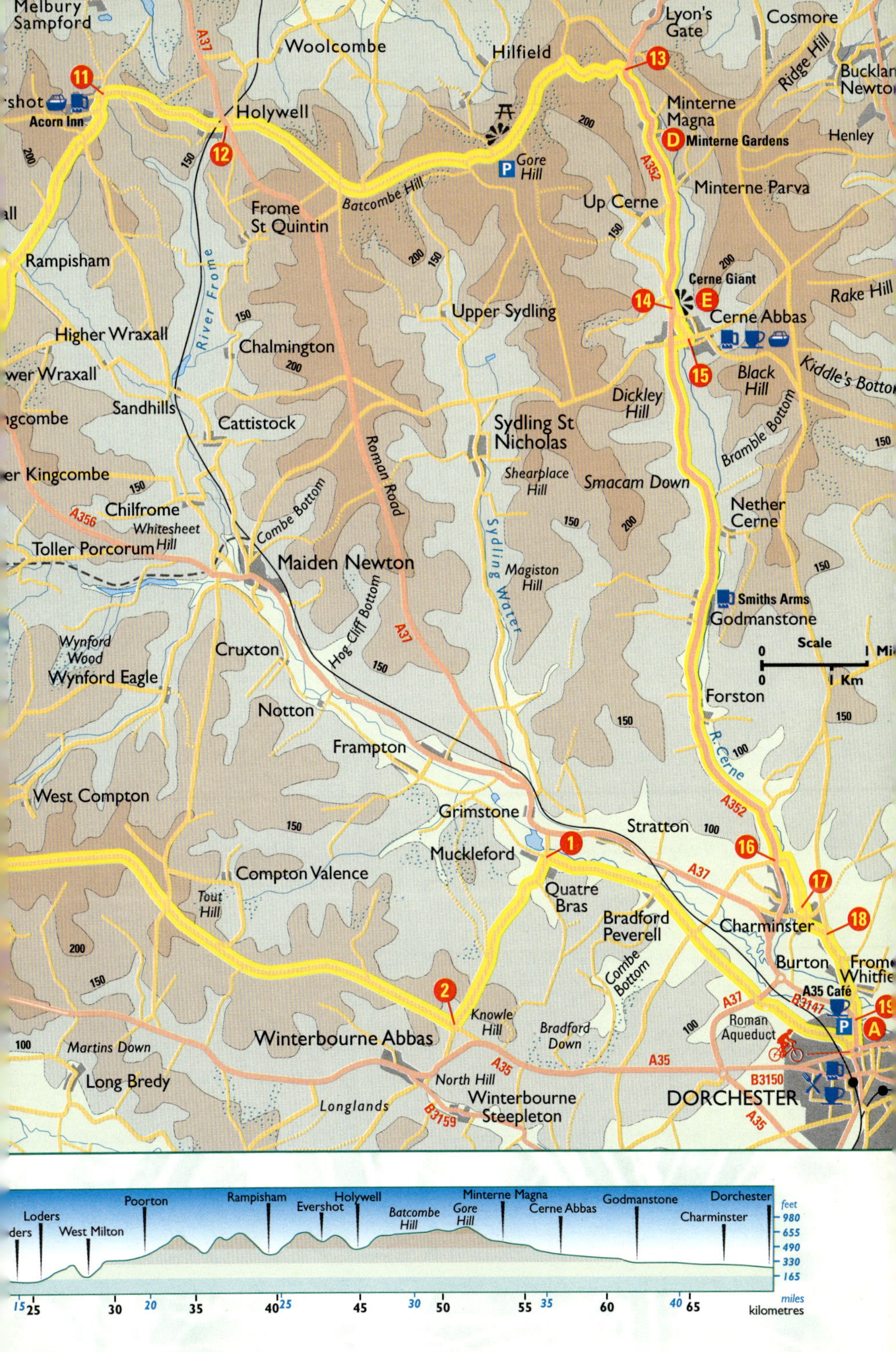

Melbury Sampford
Woolcombe
Hilfield
Lyon's Gate
Cosmore
Ridge Hill
Bucklan Newto
11
Acorn Inn
Holywell
12
13
Minterne Magna
D Minterne Gardens
Henley
Gore Hill
Minterne Parva
Batcombe Hill
Up Cerne
Frome St Quintin
Rampisham
River Frome
Cerne Giant
14
E
Cerne Abbas
Rake Hill
Upper Sydling
Higher Wraxall
Chalmington
15
Black Hill
Kiddle's Botto
wer Wraxall
Dickley Hill
Sandhills
Cattistock
Sydling St Nicholas
Bramble Bottom
er Kingcombe
Shearplace Hill
Smacam Down
Chilfrome
Combe Bottom
Roman Road
Nether Cerne
Whitesheet Hill
Toller Porcorum
Maiden Newton
Sydling Water
Magiston Hill
Smiths Arms
Godmanstone
Hog Cliff Bottom
Wynford Wood
Cruxton
Scale
0
Mi
0
Km
Wynford Eagle
Forston
Notton
Frampton
R. Cerne
West Compton
Grimstone
Stratton
1
Muckleford
16
Compton Valence
Quatre Bras
17
Tout Hill
Bradford Peverell
Charminster
18
Combe Bottom
Burton
Frome Whitfie
A35 Café
2
Knowle Hill
Bradford Down
Roman Aqueduct
A
Winterbourne Abbas
Martins Down
Long Bredy
North Hill
Winterbourne Steepleton
Longlands
DORCHESTER
A37
A352
A356
A35
B3147
B3150
B3159
Loders
Poorton
Rampisham
Evershot
Holywell
Batcombe Hill
Gore Hill
Minterne Magna
Cerne Abbas
Godmanstone
Charminster
Dorchester
ders
West Milton
feet
980
655
490
330
165
miles
kilometres

Route 21

PETERSFIELD AND THE UPPER MEON VALLEY

Route information

Distance 72km (44.5 miles)

Grade Strenuous

Terrain Mostly quiet unclassified roads. The first half of the route includes some steep hills, although none very long – unless you are sure of your cycling ability, use the low gears.

Time to allow 3–5 hours.

Getting there by car Petersfield is reached by the A3 London to Portsmouth road. Follow signs for the town centre. There are several car parks signposted. This route starts beside the railway station, where there is a pay and display car park.

Getting there by train Petersfield is well served by South West Trains on the London Waterloo to Portsmouth line. Telephone (0345) 484950 for further information.

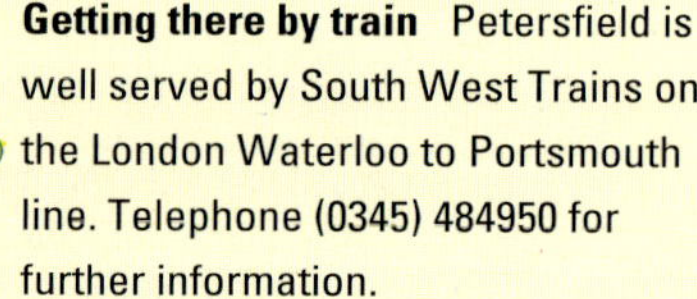

A route along quiet sunken lanes and unclassified roads, through the Upper Meon Valley and countryside designated Areas of Outstanding Natural Beauty. From Petersfield, northwards through Steep and Blackmoor, to Selborne and then south and west through West Tisted to Beacon Hill, before returning to Petersfield via East Meon and Buriton.

Places of interest along the route

A Steep

The village church here is a mix of old and new. The church contains a 13th-century font and 15th-century wooden floor as well as fine modern work including an organ case and screen from 1953. There are two windows by Laurence Whistler in memory of Edward Thomas, the World War I poet.

B Selborne, near Alton

The attractive village of Selborne is a naturalist's delight: nature reserve, Site of Special Scientific Interest, and home to Gilbert White, the famous 18th-century naturalist who immortalised the village in his book *The Natural History of Selborne*. The village church contains a fine Flemish painting of 1520. At the south end of the village, there is a small Romany museum.

C The Wakes, Selborne

The Wakes is an 18th-century country house, home to Gilbert White for most of his life. The garden, well documented through White's writing, is in the process of restoration but is already well worth a visit. Also at The Wakes is a museum dedicated to Frank Oates, who explored South America and South Africa, and Captain Lawrence Oates, valiant casualty of the ill-fated Scott expedition to the South Pole in 1912. There is a teashop and gift shop. Open end March to Christmas, daily 1100–1700; January to March, weekends only 1100–1700. Charge. Telephone (01420) 511275.

D Privett

The church at Privett, on the optional section of route, is an unaltered example of Victorian

Food and drink 

Petersfield has the normal range of shops, cafés and pubs. There is a 24-hour convenience store in Charles Street, close to the station. There are two pubs in Buriton, the Master Robert and the Five Balls, both of which serve food.

Harrow Inn, Steep
Old and attractive pub. Bar meals available. Garden.

The Cricketers, Steep
Serves snacks and meals.

Queens Hotel, Selborne
One of the few British pubs that still has a coveted Cyclists' Touring Club plaque to commend it as a cyclist-friendly pub. Reasonably-priced food.

Selborne Arms, Selborne
Real ale and a guaranteed choice of vegetarian food. Sunday lunches, but no food on Sunday evenings.

White Horse (The Pub With No Name), near East Tisted
Real ale, food and garden. Known locally as The Pub With No Name, as the pub sign went missing years ago.

George and Falcon, Warnford
Real ale and good meals.

The George, East Meon
Real ale and an excellent choice of food.

Isaac Walton, East Meon
Village pub serving local ale and bar meals.

church architecture, all the fittings dating from its construction in 1877. Designed by Arthur Blomfield and paid for by the Nicholson family (wealthy distillers), it has a 49m (160 feet) high tower. The building material came from Dumfries (the red stone), Bath (the white stone) and Ham Hill, Somerset (the yellow stone). The mosaic floor was laid by Italian craftsmen.

E East Meon

The village of East Meon is a beautiful, well-preserved village that suffers from tourists on summer weekends. The River Meon runs alongside the main street. Note the depth board beside the Isaac Walton pub, which seems to record the water level in the infant river in feet above sea level. The attractive Norman church has a handsomely carved Tournai marble font.

Route description 

From the station TR right into Station Road. Just past the large Methodist Church on your right, TL, no SP, into Tilmore Road. After 1km (0.6 mile) TL into Harrow Lane (SP Dead End) and cross over dual carriageway towards Steep.

1 TL at XR, no SP (2km/1 mile). TR, no SP, into Mill Lane. TR, SP Hawkley.

5.5 km (3.5 miles)

2 TL at TJ, SP Hawkley. SO at SP Hawkley. SO at XR, SP Newton Valence and Alton (9km/5.5 miles). TR, SP Empshott and Selborne.

3 TL at TJ with B3006, SP Alton and Selborne. TR, SP Blackmoor (16km/10 miles). TL, SP Oakhanger and Selborne. Pass The Wakes.

4 At TJ with B3006, TR into Selborne (20km/12.5 miles). Continue through Selborne.

TL, SP Newton Valence (into Gracious Street). TL at XR, no SP.

5 SO at staggered XR, SP Hawkley. TR, SP Priors Dean and Colemore (27km/17 miles). Take care on the descent. At TJ, TR, no SP. Then TL at TJ (cycleway sign) to pass the White Horse pub (no sign). At XR, SO SP Privett and descend hill. ***30km (18.5 miles)***

6 TR, SP Privett. For optional route go on about 1.5km (1 mile) to direction a. Otherwise, after about 2.5km (1.5 miles), TR, no SP. SO at XR with A32, SP West Tisted. At TJ, TR, SP West Tisted.

Optional route:

a TL at XR, SP Privett Church.

b TR at Church, SP West Tisted.

c SO at XR, SP Alton. Arrive A32 and SO, SP West Tisted. After about 1km (0.6 mile) main route joins from the right, just before West Tisted. Continue into village and direction 7.

7 In West Tisted, TL, SP Punsholt (36.5km/22.5 miles). At XR, TR, no SP. Then SO at XR, no SP.

8 Arrive A272 XR. SO, no SP. At next XR, SO (SP broken at time of writing). At foot of hill follow road as it swings left (41.5km/26 miles).

9 TL at XR, no SP (47km/29 miles). At TJ with A32, TL then TR, SP Clanfield. Cycle across Old Winchester Hill.

10 TL at XR, SP East Meon (55.5km/34.5 miles). TL then TR at foot of hill and continue to East Meon. Cycle through village and TL (by Forge) SP Frogmore. At TJ, TL, SP Buriton.

11 TR at TJ, SP Buriton (64.5km/40 miles). Continue under A3 to Buriton and continue through village (ignoring cycleway sign).

12 At TJ with B2146, TL, SP Petersfield (69km/43 miles). Continue past park and boating lake to XR in Petersfield. SO into Hylton Road. TR into Charles Street (at second small green, called The Spain) and return to Station Road and the end of the route. ***72km (44.5 miles)***

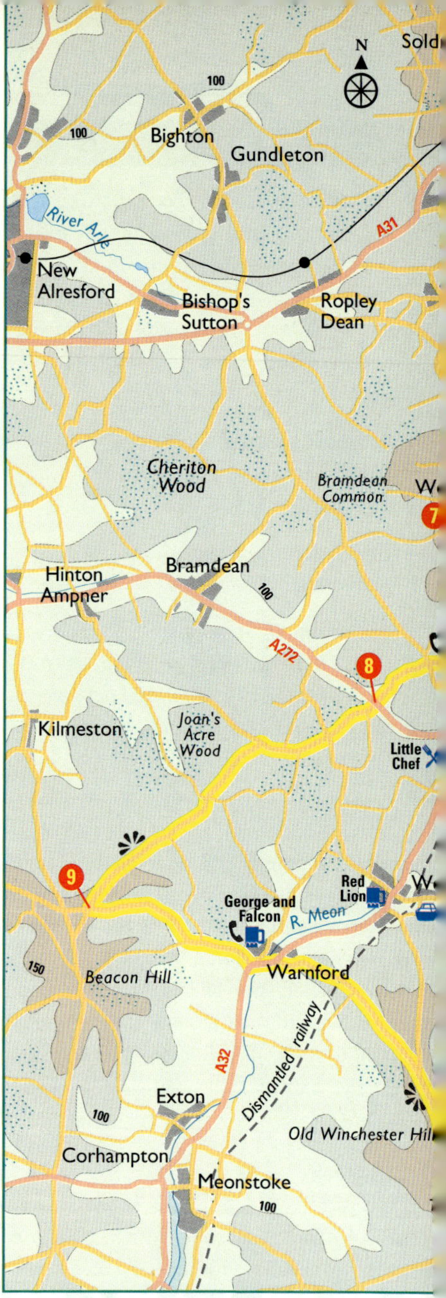

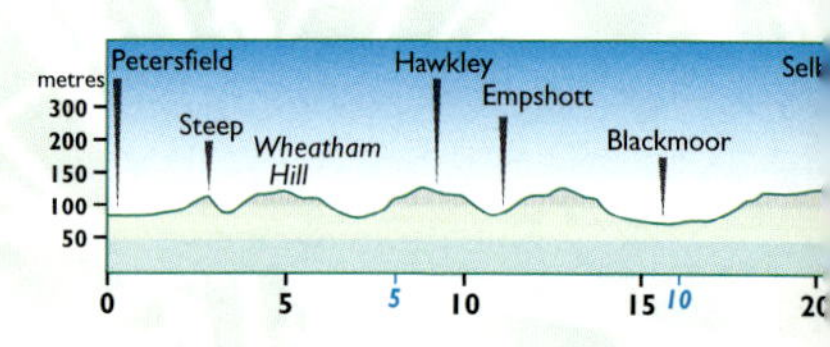

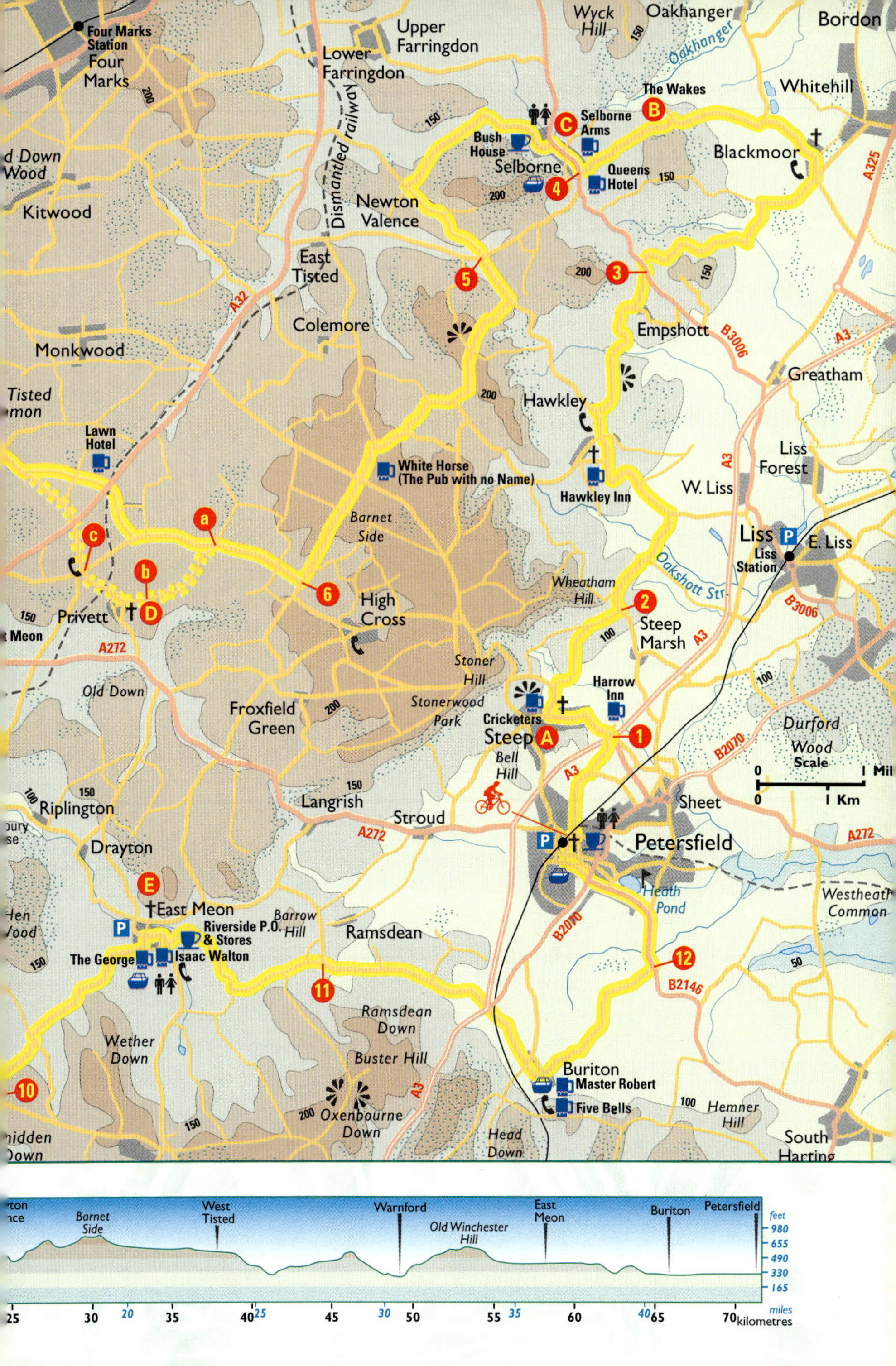
Four Marks Station
Four Marks
Upper Farringdon
Lower Farringdon
Wyck Hill
Oakhanger
Bordon
Oakhanger
The Wakes
Whitehill
Selborne Arms
Bush House
Selborne
Queens Hotel
Blackmoor
A325
Dismantled railway
d Down Wood
Kitwood
Newton Valence
East Tisted
A32
Colemore
Empshott
B3006
A3
Monkwood
Greatham
Hawkley
Tisted mon
Lawn Hotel
White Horse (The Pub with no Name)
Liss Forest
A3
Hawkley Inn
W. Liss
Barnet Side
Liss
Liss Station
E. Liss
Oakshott Str
Wheatham Hill
High Cross
Steep Marsh
B3006
Privett
Meon
A272
Stoner Hill
Harrow Inn
Old Down
Froxfield Green
Stonerwood Park
Cricketers
Steep
Durford Wood
B2070
Bell Hill
Scale
Mil
Km
A3
Sheet
Riplington
Langrish
Stroud
A272
Petersfield
A272
Drayton
Heath Pond
Westheath Common
East Meon
Riverside P.O. & Stores
Barrow Hill
Ramsdean
Hen Wood
The George
Isaac Walton
B2070
B2146
Ramsdean Down
Wether Down
Buster Hill
A3
Buriton
Master Robert
Five Bells
Oxenbourne Down
Hemner Hill
hidden Down
Head Down
South Harting
Barnet Side
West Tisted
Warnford
Old Winchester Hill
East Meon
Buriton
Petersfield
feet
980
655
490
330
165
miles
kilometres

Route **22**

BERE REGIS, BULBARROW HILL AND HARDY'S COTTAGE

Route information

Distance 74.5km (46.5 miles)

Grade Easy

Terrain Mostly undulating lanes and quiet B roads. There is one steady and gradual climb to Dorset's second highest point, Bulbarrow Hill. An optional detour (of 8.5km/5 miles) uses a short section of bridleway.

Time to allow 4–7 hours. Riding time will be increased by 1 hour if you include the off-road section.

Getting there by car Wool can be reached on the A352 from Poole in the east and from Dorchester in the west. There is a free car park (signposted) opposite the railway station.

Getting there by train Wool is on the main Waterloo to Weymouth line and has a frequent service. Telephone (0345) 484950.

From Wool the route takes you north to Bere Regis and the picturesque village of Milton Abbas, before slowly ascending to the top of Bulbarrow Hill. The magnificent views to the north are enhanced by the following 3km (2 miles) of flying descent, before a tour of sleepy north Dorset villages. The route then takes you south down the Piddle Valley to the very heartland of Hardy country. An optional off-road route visits Hardy's cottage.

Places of interest along the route

A Woolbridge

Stop and read the inscription on the plaqu here, warning that the penalty for damage t the bridge is deportation.

B Tank Museum, Bovington

Museum featuring over 250 fighting vehicle supporting artefacts, small arms and memora bilia, as well as much more. Tank firepower an mobility displays July to September, Thursday at 1200. Restaurant and gift shop. Open all yea daily 1000–1700. Telephone (01929) 405096.

C Monkey World, Wool

Monkey World was started in 1987 and is haven for chimpanzees rescued from tormen at the hands of unscrupulous entertainers c smuggled from the wild. The habitat is a natural as can be contrived and the monkey live in the freedom of large enclosures wher they can roam and climb trees freely and safe ly. At home in the centre are chimpanzees lemurs, macaques and orang-utans. Visito centre, café and gift shop. Open all year, dail 1000–1700; July and August, daily 1000–180 Charge. Telephone (0800) 456600.

D Bere Regis

Called Kingsbere by Thomas Hardy, Bere Regi is a watercress-growing village. The church c St John the Baptist is reputedly the most visite church in Dorset. The most striking features ar 12 figures, dressed in Tudor costume, that star down at the congregation. There are also th tombs of the Turbervilles, a fact Thomas Hard used in *Tess of the d'Urbervilles*.

Food and drink

Rose Mullion Restaurant, Wool
Morning coffee, lunches and cream teas.

Tea Clipper, Milton Abbas
Morning coffee and cream teas. Closed Mondays except public holidays.

Hambro Arms, Milton Abbas
Local ales and bar meals.

Baker's Folly, Bulbarrow
Restaurant.

The Antelope, Hazelbury Bryan
Local ales.

Brace of Pheasants Inn, Plush
Pub and restaurant.

The Piddle Inn, Piddletrenthide
Pub with garden and children's room.

The European Inn, Piddlehinton
Real ales in this historic inn.

E Milton Abbas

So picturesque is this thatched village it should not surprise you to find that it was in fact designed to be so. To improve the view from his country house, Lord Hambro moved the village and re-built it away to the left up the hill. In doing so, he provided a superior standard of housing for his tenants. Milton Abbey and Milton Abbey School are worth a 1km (0.6 mile) detour.

F Bulbarrow Hill

The second highest point in Dorset, with extensive views over the countryside. Bulbarrow Hill is mentioned by Hardy several times, as is much of the surrounding countryside.

G Hardy's Cottage, Higher Bockhampton

Thomas Hardy was born in this cottage in 1840. The cottage was built in 1801 by Hardy's great-grandfather and Hardy wrote *Under the Greenwood Tree* and *Far from the Madding Crowd* here. Owned by the National Trust. Open April to October, Sunday–Thursday 1100–1700. Charge. Telephone (01305) 262366.

H Ilsington House, Puddletown

A splendid mansion built in 1690 by the 7th Earl of Huntington. The house was the headquarters of the American 18th Infantry Regiment (1st division) for the D Day invasion of France during World War II. The rooms contain period furniture and decor and there is an extensive collection of paintings and sculpture of all periods. Formal and landscaped gardens. Open May to September, Wednesday and Thursday 1400–1800; August, Wednesday, Thursday, Sunday and Bank Holidays 1400–1800. Charge. Telephone (01305) 848454.

I Athelhampton House and Gardens

The house was constructed in 1845. Visitors can see the Great Hall, Great Chamber, Wine Cellar and other rooms, all beautifully furnished. Also gardens with topiary, pyramids, fountains, pavilions and rare plants. Restaurant. Open March to October, Sunday–Friday 1100–1700. Charge. Telephone (01305) 848363.

Route description

From Wool railway station cross the level crossing and take the second left across Woolbridge. Head north, SP Monkey World, passing Monkey World on your right.

1 Arrive Bere Regis and TL into main street.

2 TR (into Roke Road), SP Milborne St Andrew. ***9km (5.5 miles)***

3 TR, SP Milton Abbas, then TL at A354 (with care).

4 TR, SP Milton Abbas. ***14.5km (9 miles)***

5 TR, SP Winterborne Stickland and cycle up through the main street of Milton Abbas.

6 TL at TJ at top of village, SP Bulbarrow.

7 TL, SP Bulbarrow. ***20.5km (12.5 miles)***

8 Sharp TR at top of hill, SP Okeford Fitzpaine. Freewheel down along the ridge of the hill. ***25.5km (16 miles)***

9 TL by Royal Oak pub, SP Fifehead Neville. ***31km (19 miles)***

10 TL, SP The Fifeheads and Hazelbury Bryan.

11 TR, SP Fifehead Neville. Road is signed Unsuitable for large vehicles. Cycle through the ford and note the old bridge alongside.

12 TL at TJ, no SP. ***35.5km (22 miles)***

13 SO, SP Mappowder.

14 RHF, SP Mappowder.

15 Keep right (Hammond Street), SP Folly and Plush. ***42km (26 miles)***

16 TL, SP Piddletrenthide. ***47km (29 miles)***

17 Merge left, no SP. ***50km (31 miles)***

18 TL, SP Druce and Puddletown (56km/35 miles). Continue to direction 19, or for the off-road section continue for 2km (1 mile) to direction:

a On sharp left hand bend just before Druce, TR through metal gate. No SP, only bridleway blue arrow on post.

b Climb to top of hill on wide track and as bridleway curves to right, TL through gate onto grassy track which clears as it enters Yellowham wood. No SP, only bridleway blue arrow.

c TR onto abandoned main road.

d Cross bridge over A35.

e TL, SP Hardy's Cottage.

f At the memorial stone to Thomas Hardy, continue through Puddletown Forest, SP Puddletown.

g At junction of six tracks, follow SO on track which continues uphill.

h SO at junction with wide track.

i Join road, SP Puddletown. For Ilsington TL (the house is on your right). To visit Athelhampton House and Gardens continue on A35 for 1km (0.6 mile). Otherwise continue route at direction 20.

19 TR at TJ and then TL at traffic lights. Ilsington House is on the left. Detour 1km (0.6 mile) along main road to visit Athelhampton House and Gardens. ***59km (36.5 miles***

20 TR, SP Tincleton.

21 TR, SP Tincleton.

22 SO at staggered XR, SP Woodsford and Moreton.

23 TL, no SP.

24 SO, SP Moreton and Wool, and cycle alongside Winfrith experimental site (reactor decommissioned). ***65.5km (40.5 miles***

25 TR across railway to return to the car park in Wool . ***74.5km (46.5 miles***

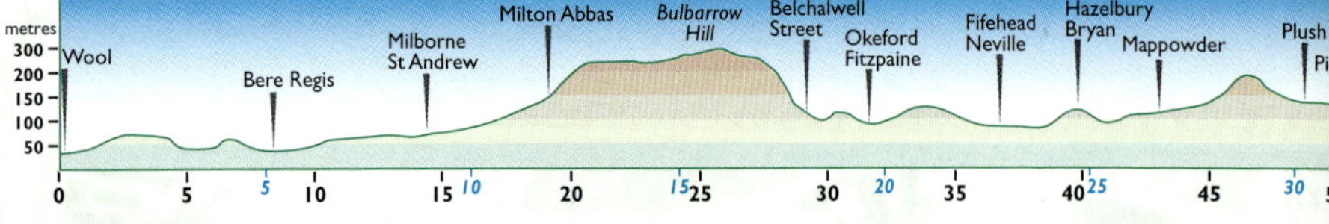

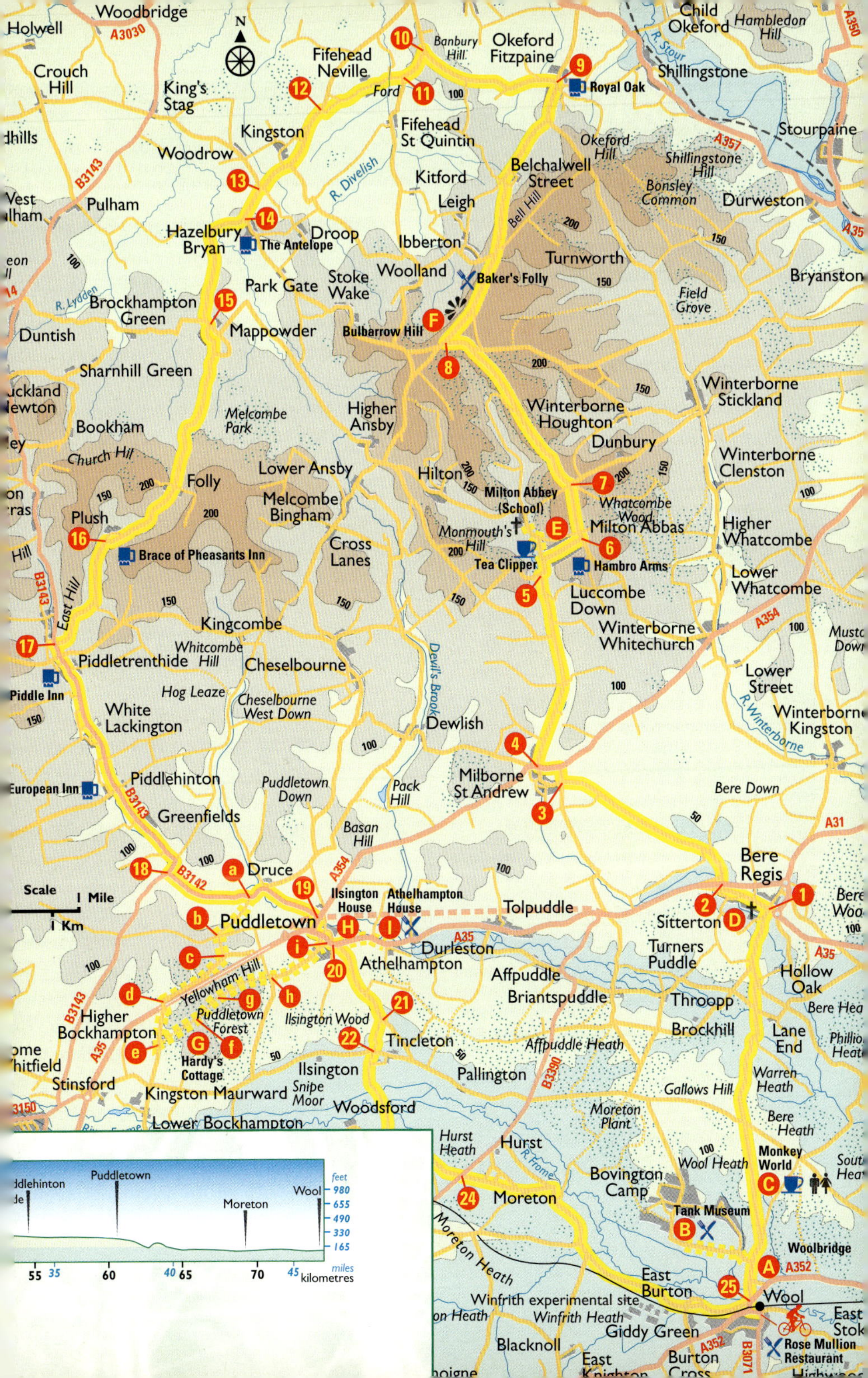

N
Woodbridge
Holwell
A3030
Crouch Hill
King's Stag
Fifehead Neville
Banbury Hill
Okeford Fitzpaine
Child Okeford
Hambledon Hill
R. Stour
A350
Shillingstone
Ford
Royal Oak
Kingston
Fifehead St Quintin
Okeford Hill
A357
Shillingstone Hill
Stourpaine
Woodrow
B3143
R. Divelish
Kitford
Belchalwell Street
Bonsley Common
Durweston
Pulham
Leigh
Bell Hill
Hazelbury Bryan
The Antelope
Droop
Ibberton
Turnworth
A35
Woolland
Baker's Folly
Bryanston
R. Lydden
Brockhampton Green
Park Gate
Stoke Wake
Field Grove
Duntish
Mappowder
Bulbarrow Hill
Sharnhill Green
Winterborne Stickland
Melcombe Park
Higher Ansby
Winterborne Houghton
Bookham
Dunbury
Church Hil
Lower Ansby
Winterborne Clenston
Folly
Hilton
Milton Abbey (School)
Melcombe Bingham
Whatcombe Wood
Plush
Monmouth's Hill
Milton Abbas
Higher Whatcombe
Brace of Pheasants Inn
Cross Lanes
Tea Clipper
Hambro Arms
Lower Whatcombe
B3143
East Hill
Luccombe Down
A354
Kingcombe
Winterborne Whitechurch
Whitcombe Hill
Piddletrenthide
Cheselbourne
Devil's Brook
Piddle Inn
Hog Leaze
Cheselbourne West Down
Lower Street
White Lackington
R.Winterborne
Dewlish
Winterborne Kingston
European Inn
Piddlehinton
Puddletown Down
Pack Hill
Milborne St Andrew
Bere Down
B3143
Greenfields
Basan Hill
A31
A354
Bere Regis
Druce
B3142
Scale
1 Mile
1 Km
Ilsington House
Athelhampton House
Tolpuddle
Sitterton
Puddletown
A35
Durleston
Turners Puddle
Athelhampton
Affpuddle
Hollow Oak
Yellowham Hill
Briantspuddle
Throopp
B3143
Higher Bockhampton
Puddletown Forest
Ilsington Wood
Brockhill
Lane End
A35
Hardy's Cottage
Tincleton
Affpuddle Heath
Warren Heath
Stinsford
Ilsington
Pallington
B3390
Gallows Hill
Kingston Maurward
Snipe Moor
Woodsford
Moreton Plant
Bere Heath
Lower Bockhampton
Hurst Heath
Hurst
R. Frome
Monkey World
Wool Heath
Bovington Camp
Moreton
Puddletown
Moreton
Wool
feet
980
655
490
330
165
55
35
60
40
65
70
45
miles
kilometres
Tank Museum
Moreton Heath
Woolbridge
A352
East Burton
Wool
Winfrith experimental site
Winfrith Heath
Giddy Green
Blacknoll
A352
East Knighton
Burton Cross
B3071
Rose Mullion Restaurant

Route 23

RURAL HAMPSHIRE – ALTON LOOP

Route information

Distance 83.5km (52 miles)

Grade Moderate

Terrain Mostly quiet byroads through rolling countryside. No major hills.

Time to allow 4–5 hours.

Getting there by car Alton can be reached from the A31 and A339 and has an extensive one-way system. There are several car parks in the town, including a pay and display car park at the railway station, from where this route starts.

Getting there by train There is a frequent service to Alton from London Waterloo and a limited service from New Alresford, via the Watercress Steam Railway. Telephone (0345) 484950 for information on mainline services and (01962) 734866 for information on the Watercress Line.

A gentle ride through rolling hills and woodland between Alton and Basingstoke. No spectacular views, but beautiful countryside.

Places of interest along the route

Alton

The market town of Alton has a history of occupation going back hundreds of years. The **Curtis Museum**, in the High Street, illustrates the history of Alton from the Romans to the present day. Open all year, Tuesday-Saturday 1000–1700. Charge. Telephone (01420) 82802. The **Allen Gallery**, Church Street, has a superb collection of pottery, temporary exhibitions and a charming garden. Opening times and telephone number as for the Curtis Museum. Admission free. **St Lawrence Church**, Church Street, is one of Hampshire's major examples of the perpendicular style, although the Norman tower dates from 1070. In 1643 the church was the scene of the final Civil War battle between the Roundheads and the Cavaliers in Alton. Bullets and other relics can be found in the church – the main doors and walls still bear scars from the battle. South of the railway station (reached via Papermill Lane) is **Kings Pond** – a small nature reserve, with a lake fed by the River Wey, and home to many species of wild flowers, birds and waterfowl. The **Flood Meadows**, off Tanhouse Lane, are 6ha (15 acres) of natural grassland and flood meadow. The River Wey flows through the site, where there are remains of watercress beds. For those going to Alton by car, 17th-century **Chawton House**, off the A31 southwest of Alton, was the home of Jane Austen from 1809–1817, and where she wrote and revised her six great novels. Garden and bookshop. Open March to December, daily 1100–1630; January to February, weekends 1100– 1630. Charge. Telephone (01420) 83262.

Route description 

Leave Alton railway station and TR into Ansty Road. TL, SP Holybourne and Binsted. SO at XR to Binsted.

1 TL, SP Isington and Bentley.

5.5km (3.5 miles)

2 Arrive Isington and TL, SP Froyle and Alton. Continue to Lower Froyle where TR, SP Well (opposite Prince of Wales pub).

3 TL at XR in Well, SP Long Sutton (13km/8 miles). TR, SP Odiham and continue into Odiham.

4 TL at TJ in Odiham (19.5km/12 miles). TR at junction with B3349, SP Hook, then TL, SP Greywell. TL at TJ, SP Upton Grey and Herriard (21.5km/13.5miles) and continue to and then through Upton Grey to A339.

5 SO at XR with A339 (30.5km/19 miles). Continue to Axford.

6 At TJ with B3046 in Axford, TR then TL, SP North Waltham. ***37km (23 miles)***

7 Cycle under M3. Cross A30 (TL then TR with care). Continue past Wheatsheaf pub and on to North Waltham.

8 Take LHF in North Waltham, by church, SP Overton.

9 TL at XR, SP Micheldever Station (45.5km/28.5 miles). At next junction, bear left.

10 TR at TJ (49.5km/31 miles). TL at next TJ, under A303, and continue SO. TL at XR, SP Station. Then TR at XR, SP West Stratton and continue through village.

11 TR at TJ with A33, no SP (55.5km/34.5 miles). TL, SP East Stratton. In East Stratton, bear right by church.

Food and drink 

Alton and Odiham have numerous pubs, cafés and shops. There are convenience stores in North Waltham and Medstead. The following pubs are en route and offer bar meals:

- **The Anchor, Lower Froyle**
- **Prince of Wales, Lower Froyle**
- **The Chequers, Well**
- **Hoddington Arms, Upton Grey**
- **The Plough, East Stratton**
- **Three Horseshoes, Bighton**
- **Castle of Comfort, Medstead**

12 SO at XR, SP Itchen Abbas. TL, no SP, to Abbotstone. In Abbotstone keep right, SP Bighton and Alresford.

13 TR at TJ, no SP (continue into New Alresford for refreshments if required). To continue route, TL SP Bighton.

14 At TJ in Bighton, TR then TL, SP Medstead.

15 Arrive Medstead (75km/46.5 miles). TR, SP Alton, and follow SP to A339.

16 TR onto A339 (with care), SP Alton (80.5km/50 miles). Ignore SP Town Centre and at mini roundabout SO. TL onto one-way system. TR at TJ by church and either follow SP Cycleway to station or, TL at TJ and return to station. ***83.5km (52 miles)***

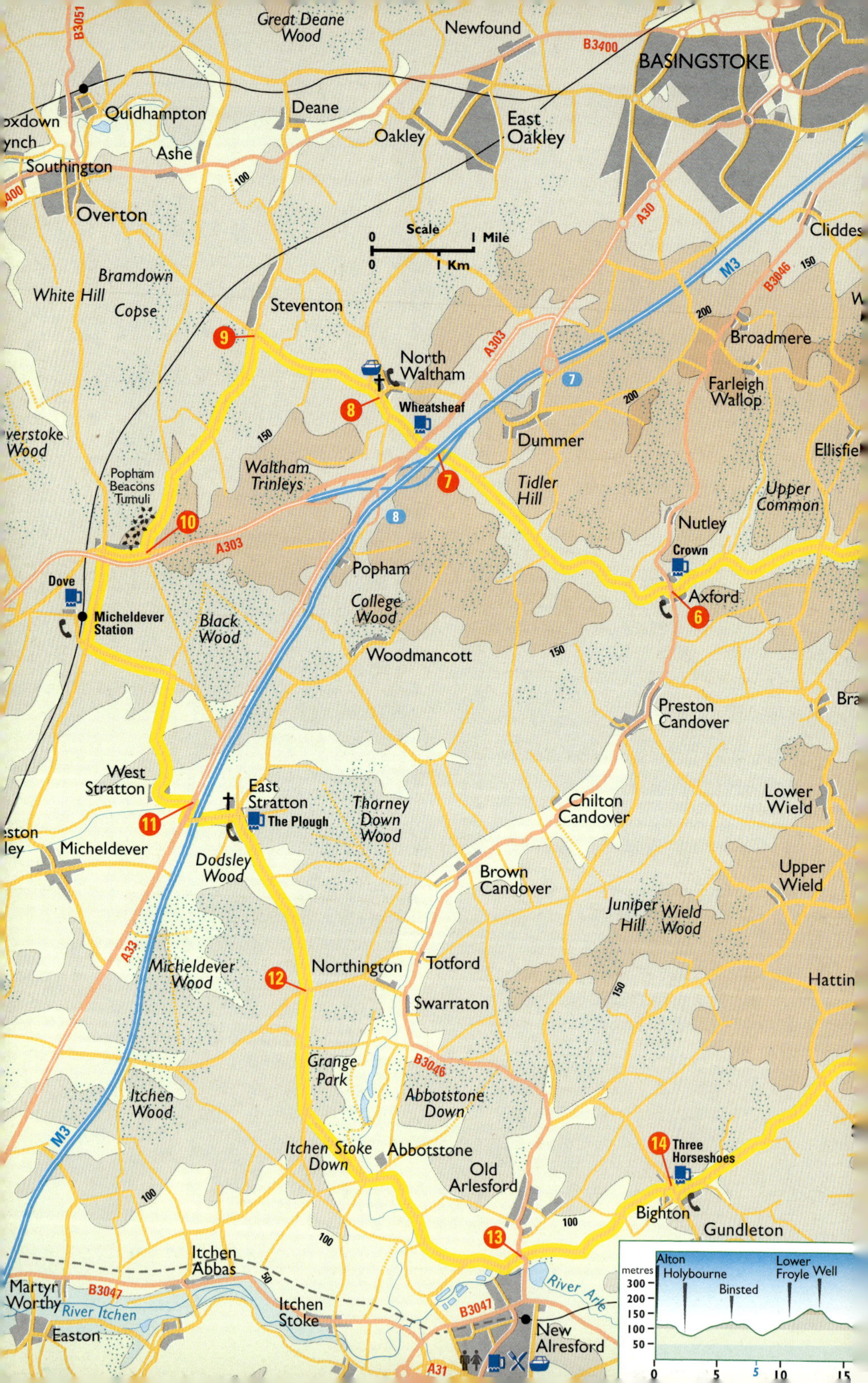

BASINGSTOKE
Great Deane Wood
Newfound
Quidhampton
Deane
Oakley
East Oakley
Southington
Ashe
Overton
Scale
0
1 Mile
0
1 Km
Bramdown
White Hill
Copse
Steventon
North Waltham
Wheatsheaf
Broadmere
Farleigh Wallop
Dummer
Popham Beacons Tumuli
Waltham Trinleys
Tidler Hill
Upper Common
Nutley
Crown
Axford
Dove
Micheldever Station
Popham
College Wood
Black Wood
Woodmancott
Preston Candover
West Stratton
East Stratton
The Plough
Thorney Down Wood
Chilton Candover
Lower Wield
Micheldever
Dodsley Wood
Brown Candover
Upper Wield
Juniper Hill
Wield Wood
Micheldever Wood
Northington
Totford
Swarraton
Grange Park
Abbotstone Down
Itchen Wood
Itchen Stoke Down
Abbotstone
Old Arlesford
Three Horseshoes
Bighton
Gundleton
Itchen Abbas
Martyr Worthy
River Itchen
Easton
Itchen Stoke
New Alresford
River Arle
M3
A303
A30
A33
A31
B3046
B3047
B3400
B3051
6
7
8
9
10
11
12
13
14
metres
300
200
150
100
50
Alton
Holybourne
Binsted
Lower Froyle
Well
0
5
10
15

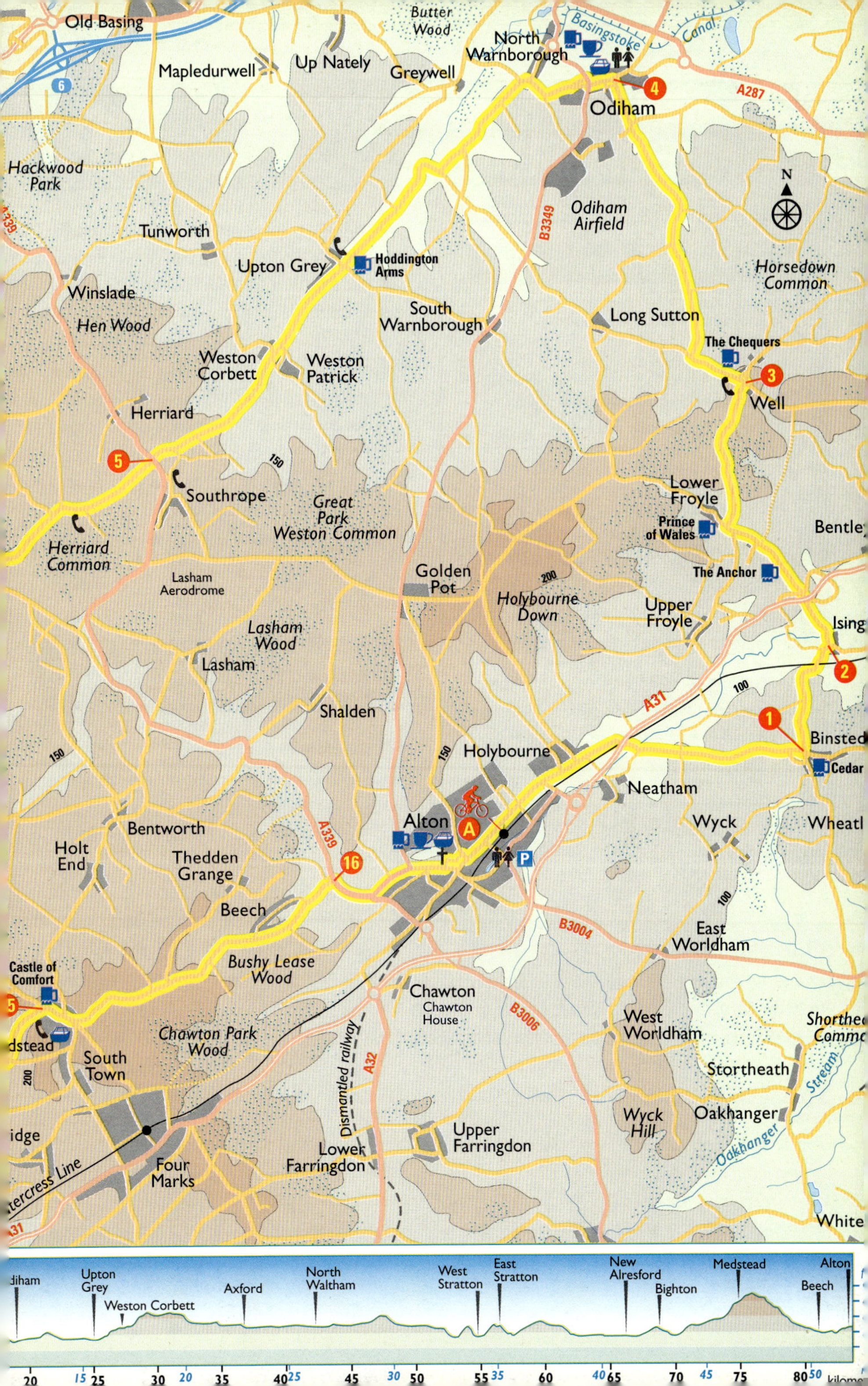

Old Basing
Mapledurwell
Up Nately
Butter Wood
Greywell
North Warnborough
Basingstoke Canal
Odiham
A287
Hackwood Park
Tunworth
Upton Grey
Hoddington Arms
B3349
Odiham Airfield
Horsedown Common
Winslade
Hen Wood
South Warnborough
Long Sutton
The Chequers
Weston Corbett
Weston Patrick
Well
Herriard
Southrope
Great Park
Weston Common
Lower Froyle
Prince of Wales
Herriard Common
Lasham Aerodrome
Golden Pot
Holybourne Down
The Anchor
Upper Froyle
Lasham Wood
Lasham
Shalden
A31
Holybourne
Binsted
Cedar
Neatham
Alton
Wyck
Bentworth
Holt End
Thedden Grange
A339
Beech
B3004
East Worldham
Bushy Lease Wood
Castle of Comfort
Chawton
Chawton House
B3006
West Worldham
Chawton Park Wood
South Town
Dismantled railway
A32
Stortheath
Upper Farringdon
Wyck Hill
Oakhanger
Oakhanger Stream
Lower Farringdon
Four Marks
Upton Grey
Weston Corbett
Axford
North Waltham
West Stratton
East Stratton
New Alresford
Bighton
Medstead
Alton
Beech

Route 24

NEW FOREST RANDONNEE – THE GRIDIRON

Route information

Distance 100km (62 miles)

Grade Moderate

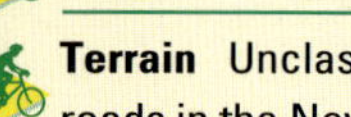

Terrain Unclassified, flat minor roads in the New Forest.

Time to allow 5–8 hours.

Getting there by car The route starts in Brockenhurst (on the A337) in the centre of the New Forest. There is a 40mph speed limit on most roads in the New Forest and parking is restricted to designated places.

Getting there by train Brockenhurst is on the main Waterloo to Weymouth line and has a frequent service. Telephone (0345) 484950.

Two fast main roads cross the New Forest, and a few other roads in the centre of the region tend to be heavy with traffic. This route circles the New Forest and makes for pleasant cycling – from Brockenhurst across the southernmost coastal sections of the New Forest to the old shipyard town of Bucklers Hard, before heading north and crossing through harsher de-forested land in the north of the forest. The route goes through the string of gentle villages on the western edge of the forest to Ringwood, before returning to Brockenhurst. Ponies and cattle roam everywhere and cattle grids are a frequent feature of this ride. Be careful of them all.

Special note: this route is used by the local CTC each October for a popular randonnée known as the Gridiron, in which hundreds of cyclists participate. It is also offered as a permanent randonnée – you can add an extra dimension to your cycling and become a real randonneur by registering and paying a small fee. You will be issued with a brevet card upon which you obtain check stamps to prove your ride. This is then authorised and returned to you to keep. For information, send a SAE to GRIDIRON, 7 Cotes Avenue, Parkstone, Poole, Dorset, BH14 OND.

Places of interest along the route

A The New Forest

The New Forest was new in the 12th century when King Rufus decided to use it for hunting. He died in a hunting accident, commemorated at the Rufus Stone. Nowadays, the region is neither new and largely not a forest, having been almost completely denuded of trees (for shipbuilding) during the Napoleonic wars. Consequently, the character of the landscape has changed completely. It is still impressive, but very much the product of human intervention. The forest is popular with cyclists, but can become uncomfortably saturated with visitors in the summer. The wide open spaces encourage sightseeing from the comfort of a slowly cruising car with a consequent less than perfect attention to the road. Erratic and unpredictable driving should be expected. The route followed here avoids the worst of these roads as much as possible.

B Bucklers Hard

The 18th-century village of Bucklers Hard is largely preserved. This is where the ships were made for Nelson's fleet from oak taken from the New Forest – most of the ancient oak was denuded at this time. **Maritime Museum**, reflecting the village's shipbuilding tradition and **cottage** recreating 18th-century life. Museum and cottage open all year, daily 1000–1700. Charge. Telephone (01590) 616203.

C Beaulieu

A picturesque village situated just where the river opens up into a wide navigable waterway. Lord Beaulieu's residence (**Palace House**) can be seen across the lake and the **National Motor Museum** is to the north of the village. House and museum open all year, daily 1000–1700. Charge. Telephone (01590) 612123.

D Owl Sanctuary, Crow

A sanctuary and bird hospital dedicated to returning injured birds to the wild. Funded by visitors and by donations. Lectures and flying displays held daily. Café. Open March to November, daily 1000–1700. Charge. Telephone (01425) 476487.

Food and drink

Brockenhurst and Burley have several cafés and restaurants. There are convenience stores in Ibsley and Poulner.

Red Lion Pub, Boldre
Local ales and bar meals.

Master Builders Inn, Bucklers Hard
Local ales, bar meals, restaurant and village shop.

Old Bake House Tearooms, Beaulieu
Tea, coffee and meals.

Lamb Inn, Normansland
Local ales, bar meals and snacks.

Three Lions Restaurant, Stuckton
Lunches and dinners.

Alice Lyle Inn, Ibsley
Real ales, garden and play area.

New Forest

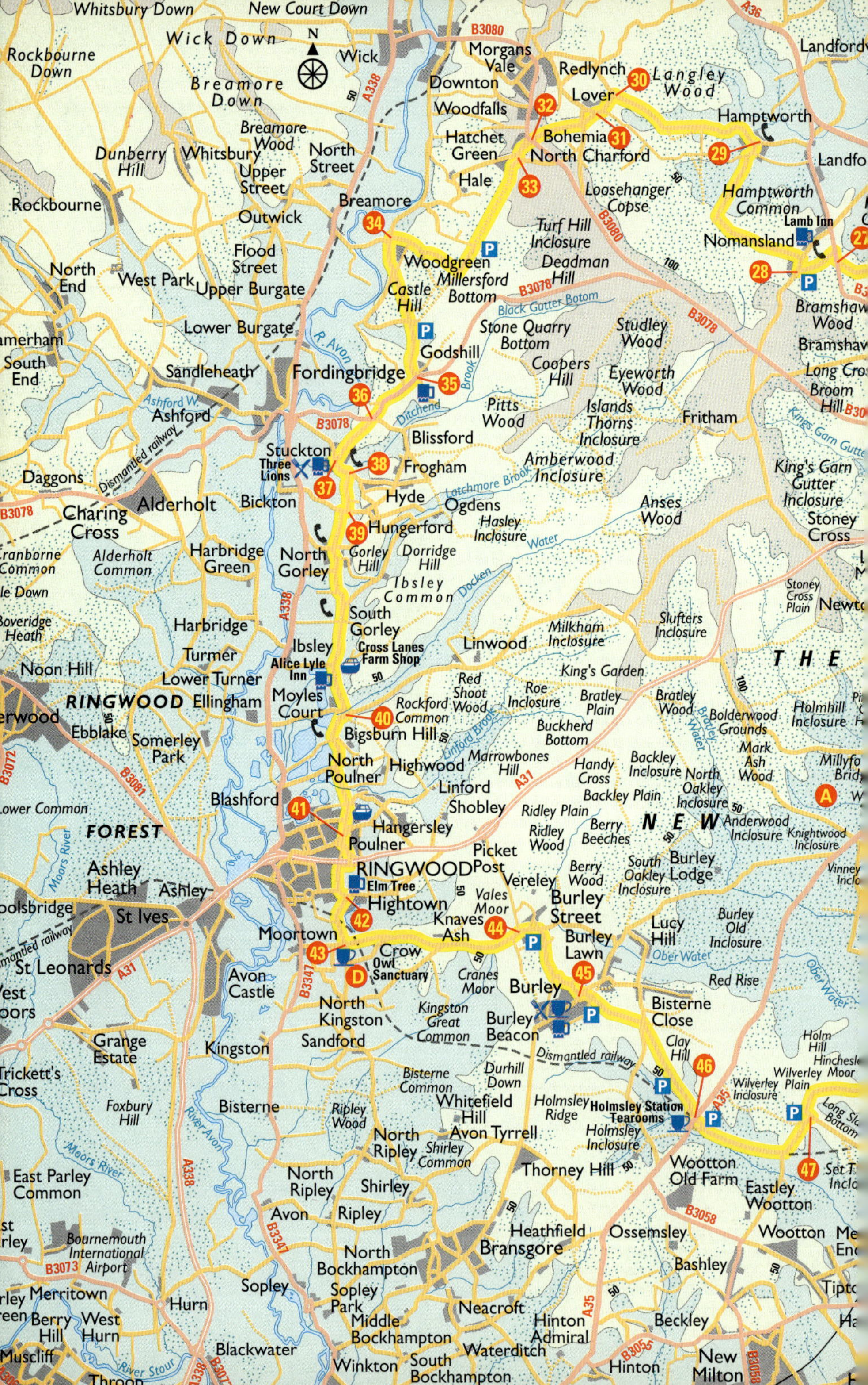

Whitsbury Down
New Court Down
A36
Landford
B3080
Wick Down
Rockbourne Down
Wick
Morgans Vale
Redlynch
Langley Wood
Breamore Down
Downton
Lover
30
Woodfalls
32
Hamptworth
Breamore Wood
Bohemia
31
Dunberry Hill
Whitsbury
North Street
Hatchet Green
North Charford
29
Landford
Upper Street
Hale
33
Loosehanger Copse
Hamptworth Common
Rockbourne
Breamore
Outwick
34
Turf Hill Inclosure
Lamb Inn
Nomansland
27
Flood Street
Woodgreen
Deadman Hill
North End
West Park
Upper Burgate
Castle Hill
Millersford Bottom
B3078
28
Bramshaw Wood
Black Gutter Botom
Studley Wood
B3078
Lower Burgate
Stone Quarry Bottom
Bramshaw
South End
R. Avon
Godshill
Sandleheath
Fordingbridge
Coopers Hill
Eyeworth Wood
Long Cross
Broom Hill
35
36
Brook
Ashford W.
Ashford
Ditchend
Pitts Wood
Islands Thorns Inclosure
Fritham
B3078
Kings Garn Gutter
Blissford
Dismantled railway
Stuckton
Three Lions
38
Frogham
Amberwood Inclosure
King's Garn Gutter Inclosure
Daggons
37
Latchmore Brook
Hyde
Ogdens
B3078
Alderholt
Bickton
Anses Wood
Charing Cross
39
Hungerford
Hasley Inclosure
Stoney Cross
Water
Alderholt Common
Harbridge Green
North Gorley
Gorley Hill
Dorridge Hill
Ibsley Common
Docken
Stoney Cross Plain
Newt
A338
South Gorley
Harbridge
Slufters Inclosure
Milkham Inclosure
Ibsley
Cross Lanes Farm Shop
Linwood
Turmer
THE
Noon Hill
Alice Lyle Inn
King's Garden
Lower Turner
50
Red Shoot Wood
Roe Inclosure
Bratley Plain
Bratley Wood
100
RINGWOOD
Ellingham
Moyles Court
Rockford Common
Bratley Water
Bolderwood Grounds
Holmhill Inclosure
40
Ebblake
Bigsburn Hill
Linford Brook
Buckherd Bottom
Mark Ash Wood
Somerley Park
Marrowbones Hill
Handy Cross
Backley Inclosure
North Oakley Inclosure
Millyford Bridge
North Poulner
Highwood
A31
B3072
B3081
Linford
Backley Plain
A
Blashford
Shobley
Ridley Plain
Anderwood Inclosure
Lower Common
41
Berry Beeches
NEW
Knightwood Inclosure
FOREST
Hangersley
Ridley Wood
Moors River
Poulner
Picket Post
South Oakley Inclosure
Burley Lodge
Vinney Inclo
Ashley Heath
Ashley
RINGWOOD
Vereley
Berry Wood
Elm Tree
Vales Moor
Burley Street
Hightown
Lucy Hill
Burley Old Inclosure
St Ives
42
Knaves Ash
44
Burley Lawn
Dismantled railway
Moortown
Crow
43
Owl Sanctuary
D
Oberwater
Ober Water
St Leonards
A31
Cranes Moor
45
Burley
Red Rise
Avon Castle
B3347
North Kingston
Kingston Great Common
Bisterne Close
Burley Beacon
Holm Hill
Grange Estate
Kingston
Sandford
Clay Hill
Dismantled railway
46
Wilverley Plain
Bisterne Common
Durhill Down
Wilverley Inclosure
Bisterne
Whitefield Hill
Holmsley Ridge
Holmsley Station Tearooms
Foxbury Hill
Ripley Wood
A35
Long Slade Bottom
North Ripley
Avon Tyrrell
Holmsley Inclosure
River Avon
Shirley Common
47
Moors River
Thorney Hill
Wootton Old Farm
East Parley Common
North Ripley
Shirley
Eastley Wootton
A338
B3058
Avon
Ripley
B3347
Heathfield
Ossemsley
Wootton
Bournemouth International Airport
Bransgore
Bashley
North Bockhampton
B3073
Merritown
Sopley
Sopley Park
Hurn
Neacroft
A35
Berry Hill
West Hurn
Middle Bockhampton
Hinton Admiral
Beckley
Muscliff
Blackwater
Waterditch
B3055
New Milton
River Stour
Winkton
South Bockhampton
Hinton
B3058
Throop
A338
B3073

Sherfield English
Squab Wood
Cupernham
Hiltingbury
Romsey
Halterworth
Flexford
Woodington
East Wellow
Hall Copse
Burnt Grove
Whitenap
Baddesley Common
Chandler's Ford
Fryern Hill
North Baddesley
Nutburn
Great Covert
Plaitford
West Wellow
Kentford Lake
Embley Wood
Yewtree Copse
River Test
Ashfield
Tanner's Brook
Chilworth
Hut Wood
EASTLEIGH
West Wellow Common
Blackhill
Shelley Common
Ridge
Toothill
R. Blackwater
Ham Lake
Canada
Foxbury Plantation
Lee
Nightingale Wood
Upton
North Stoneham
Chilworth Common
Penn Common
Half Moon Common
Paultons Park
Wigley
Ower
Moorcourt
Rownhams
Lord's Wood
Furzley
Cadnam River
Hillstreet
Nursling
Lord's Hill
Bassett
Swaythling
Stagbury Hill
Hillyfields
Aldermoor
Cadnam Common
Newbridge
Copythorne
Calmore
Shirley Warren
Highfield
Bitterne Park
Wimpson
Southampton Common
Winsor
Redbridge
Shirley
Portswood
St. Denys
Bignel Wood
Cadnam
Netley Marsh
TOTTON
Bartley
Millbrook
SOUTHAMPTON
Brokenford
Northam
Shave Wood
Goldenhayes
Ashurst Bridge
Eling
River Itchen
Itchen
Brockis Hill
Woodlands
Hounsdown
Ashurst
Trotts
Rooksgreen
Cracknore Hard
Woolston
Busketts Lawn Inclosure
Bartley River
Minstead
Colbury
Langley Wood
RIVER TEST
Manor Wood
Marchwood
Churchplace Inclosure
Rushpole Wood
Pikeshill
Staplewood Hill
Marchwood Park
SOUTHAMPTON WATER
Mallard Wood
Longdown Inclosure
Lyndhurst
Fox Hill
Beaulieu R.
Peel Hill
Dibden
Applemore
White Moor
Matley Heath
Goose Green
B3056
Hythe
Pondhead Inclosure
Matley Bog
Dibden Bottom
Langdown
Clayhill
Black Down
Yew Tree Heath
Bank
FOREST
Dibden Purlieu
Gritnam Wood
Butts Lawn
Park Hill
Denny Wood
Kings Hat Inclosure
The Noads
Buttsash
Whitley Wood
Parkhill Inclosure
New Park Plantation
Highland Water
Hollands Wood
Beaulieu Heath
Fawley Inclosure
Hardley
Poundhill Heath
Stubby Copse Inclosure
Denny Lodge Inclosure
Hartford Heath
Little Holbury
Bolderford Bridge
Pignal Inclosure
Rowbarrow
Tantany Wood
Stonyford Pond
Oil Refinery
Ober Heath
Perrywood Haseley Inclosure
Balmerlawn
Frame Wood
Stubbs Wood
Holbury
Black Knowl
Beachern Wood
New Copse Inclosure
Frame Heath Inclosure
Moon Hill
Hill Top
Motor Museum
Moonhills Copse
Otterwood
Brockenhurst
Stockley Inclosure
Hatchet Gate
Beaulieu
Blackfield
North Weirs
Round Hill
B3055
Old Bake House Tearooms
Kings Copse Inclosure
South Weirs
Brockenhurst Park
Hatchet Pond
Bunkers Hill
Bailey's Hard
Spearbed Copse
Newlands Copse
Hatchet Moor
Gilbury Hard
Setley
B3054
East Boldre
Keeping
West Common
Beaulieu Heath
Beaulieu River
Setley Plain
Sandy Down
Ashen Wood
Bucklers Hard
Exbury
Newhouse Copse
Tylers Copse
Master Builders Inn
Haxland Pits
Lower Exbury
Battramsley
Pilley Bailey
Crockford Bridge
Newlands Plantation
Coopers Wood
Lepe
Battramsley Cross
Boldre
Bull Hill
Norley Inclosure
St. Leonards Grange
Durns Town
Shirley Holms
Red Lion
Pilley
Horsemoor Copse
Gins
Norleywood
Mount Pleasant
Portmore
East End
Bergerie
Needs Ore Point
St. Rose
Vicars Hill
Thorns Copse
Sowley Pond
Scale
Mile
Km
Lower Buckland
Buckland
Walhampton
South Baddesley
Upper Pennington
LYMINGTON

Route description

From the railway level crossing gates in Brockenhurst, take the LHF into the town (heading southwest). Cross cattlegrid, your first of the day, and TL at XR into Sway Road, SP Sway and New Milton. Continue along tree-lined road and over railway bridge.

1 TR, SP Sway. Cycle under railway bridges and up the rise.

2 TL, SP Lymington. Continue to cattle grid and A337.

3 TR onto A337 (with care) and after about 100 metres TL, sharply, into Lower Sandy Down Road. Continue down to TJ.

4 TR at TJ, no SP (no warning of junction either!).

5 TL at Red Lion pub, SP Lymington.
7.5km (5 miles)

6 TR, SP Vicars Hill and South Baddesley.

7 Keep left by the schools.

8 SO at XR with B3054, SP South Baddesley.

9 LHF, no SP.

10 TR at TJ. TL at next TJ (South Baddesley School) into South Baddesley Road. Continue to cattle grid. ***12km (7.5 miles)***

11 RHF at TJ, SP Sowley.

12 TR at TJ, SP Beaulieu.

13 TR, SP Bucklers Hard (21km/13 miles). Keep left in village and continue on the road north.

14 TR, SP Lyndhurst, and TR at TJ with B3054, SP Beaulieu. Go down hill which swings to the left. The picturesque village is on the right and a little further on is the Motor Museum. ***25km (15.5 miles)***

Beaulieu Palace House

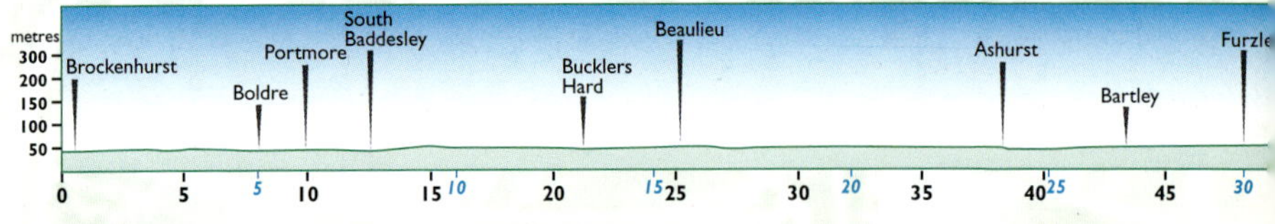

15 TR, SP Totton.

16 SO and then cross cattle grid, pass pub.

17 TL, SP Colbury, and continue through wooded area.

18 TL onto A35 for 1.5km (1 mile), through Ashurst and over the railway bridge.

38km (23.5 miles)

19 TR immediately after railway bridge, SP Woodlands.

20 TL at TJ, SP Bartley.

21 TL at Bartley Church.

22 TL at TJ and TR at shop, no SP, into New Inn Road.

23 SO at XR with A336 (with care), SP Copythorne.

24 TL, SP Newbridge and Ower, into Pollards Moor Road.

25 SO at XR with A31 and pass under M27.

46km (28.5 miles)

26 SO at XR, SP Nomansland.

27 TR at TJ and immediately TL, no SP.

28 TR at TJ then, by the Lamb Inn, turn into South Lane and cross cattle grid.

53km (33 miles)

29 TL, SP Redlynch, and continue through Langley Wood.

30 TL, SP Lover (easily missed, take care).

60km (37.5 miles)

31 LHF, SP Woodfalls.

32 SO at XR with B3080 then TL, SP Hale.

33 Cross cattle grid and LHF, no SP.

67km (41.5 miles)

34 TL at TJ to Godshill.

35 TR at TJ with B3078, by pub.

36 Where B3078 turns right, take second left, SP Stuckton.

37 TL at TJ by pub.

38 TR, SP North Gorley.

39 TR at TJ and immediately TL, SP North Gorley. Continue through North Gorley and on past South Gorley.

40 Cross ford and SO (bearing right), SP Ringwood. Keep SO through next ford, SP Poulner.

79km (49 miles)

41 TL, no SP, then TL, no SP. TR, SP Hightown. Cross A31 on bridge and TR, SP Hightown, at mini-roundabout. Then TL, SP Owl Sanctuary. (Careful not to join A31.)

42 TR by Elm Tree Pub, SP Burley.

43 TL at TJ, SP Burley.

44 TR at TJ, SP Burley Street.

87km (54 miles)

45 Cycle up through village and TL at memorial, then bear right, SP Brockenhurst.

46 Cross under A35 by Holmsley Station Tearooms and keep left at next junction.

93km (58 miles)

47 Keep left, no SP.

48 TR and through watersplash to return to station and the end of the route.

100km (62 miles)

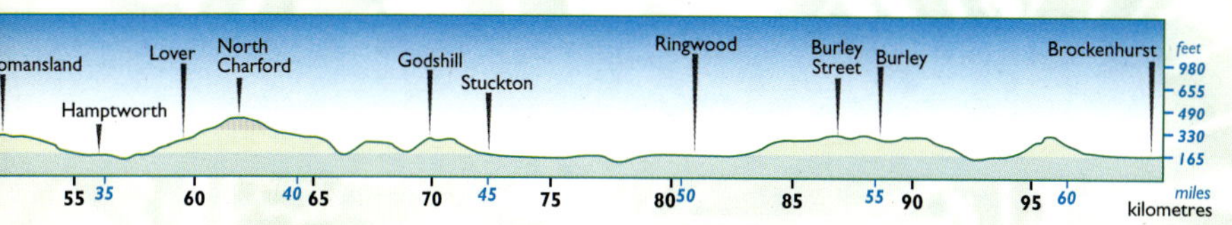

Route 25

SHERBORNE TO DORCHESTER – A GRANDE RANDONNEE

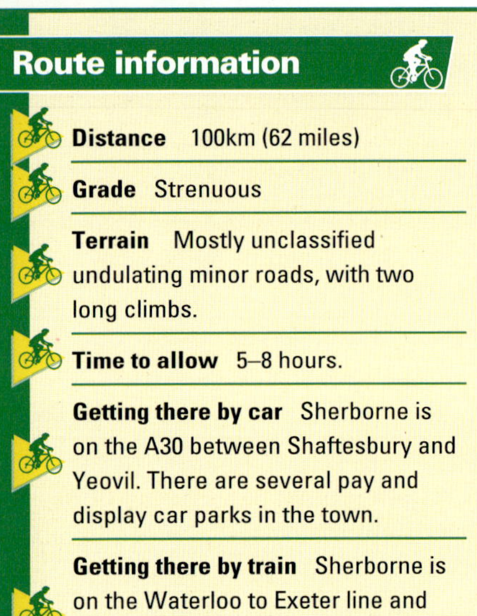

Route information

Distance 100km (62 miles)

Grade Strenuous

Terrain Mostly unclassified undulating minor roads, with two long climbs.

Time to allow 5–8 hours.

Getting there by car Sherborne is on the A30 between Shaftesbury and Yeovil. There are several pay and display car parks in the town.

Getting there by train Sherborne is on the Waterloo to Exeter line and has a frequent service. Telephone (0345) 484950 for information.

From Sherborne westwards along quiet country lanes to the Sutton Bingham reservoir. The route then turns south along the Frome valley to just north of Dorchester, before climbing Bulbarrow Hill. Onwards through the flat lands of north Dorset villages, before returning to Sherborne along the exact line of the Dorset and Somerset border.

Places of interest along the route

A Sherborne

Sherborne is a perfect English country town with many medieval buildings. From the Saxon *scir burne*, the place of the clear stream, Sherborne is sheltered in a valley by the River Yeo and has the air of a cathedral city with **Sherborne Abbey**, founded by Bishop Aldhelm (St Adhelm) in 705 AD. The first place of worship on this site was almost certainly a church, before the cathedral was constructed. The

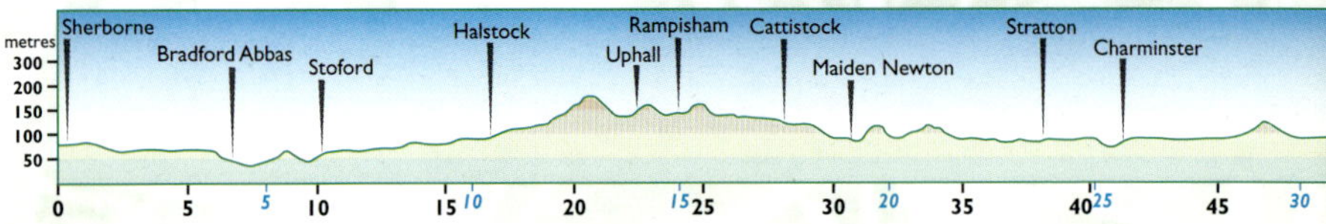

church has been rebuilt several times, in the eleventh, twelfth and thirteenth centuries. Bought by the people of Sherborne after the dissolution of the monasteries in 1539, it was made their parish church. The exterior and interior of the building are impressive and beautiful. Bookstall. Open all year, May to September 0800–1800; October to April 0800–1600. Admission free (donations requested). Telephone (01935) 812452. The 13th-century **Almshouses** in Trendle Street are still lived in today, and the associated chapel and records are open May to September, daily 1400–1600. Charge. **Sherborne Old Castle**, to the east of the town, is of Norman origin. Originally built as a fortified palace, the castle was home to the Bishop of Salisbury and Abbot of Sherborne. Sir Walter Raleigh leased the castle from Queen Elizabeth, and built Sherborne Lodge in the grounds. Open end March to October, daily 1000–1800; November to early March, Wednesday–Sunday 1000–1600. **Sherborne Castle** was built by Sir Walter Raleigh in 1594, originally as a hunting lodge, and has been the home of the Digby family since 1617. Fascinating architecture and furnishings, and priceless collections of paintings, porcelain and family treasures. The castle is surrounded by a lake, lawns and parkland. Restaurant and gift shop. Open Easter to September, Thursdays, weekends and Bank Holiday Mondays 1330–1700. Charge. Telephone (01935) 813182.

B Dorchester

There is much to see and do in Dorchester. See Route 3 for information.

Dorset countryside

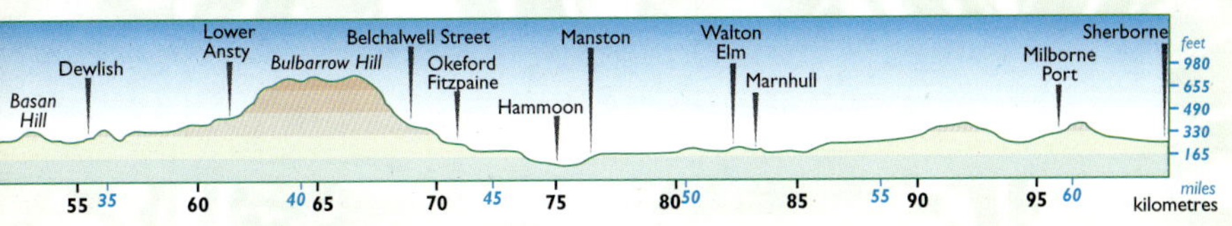

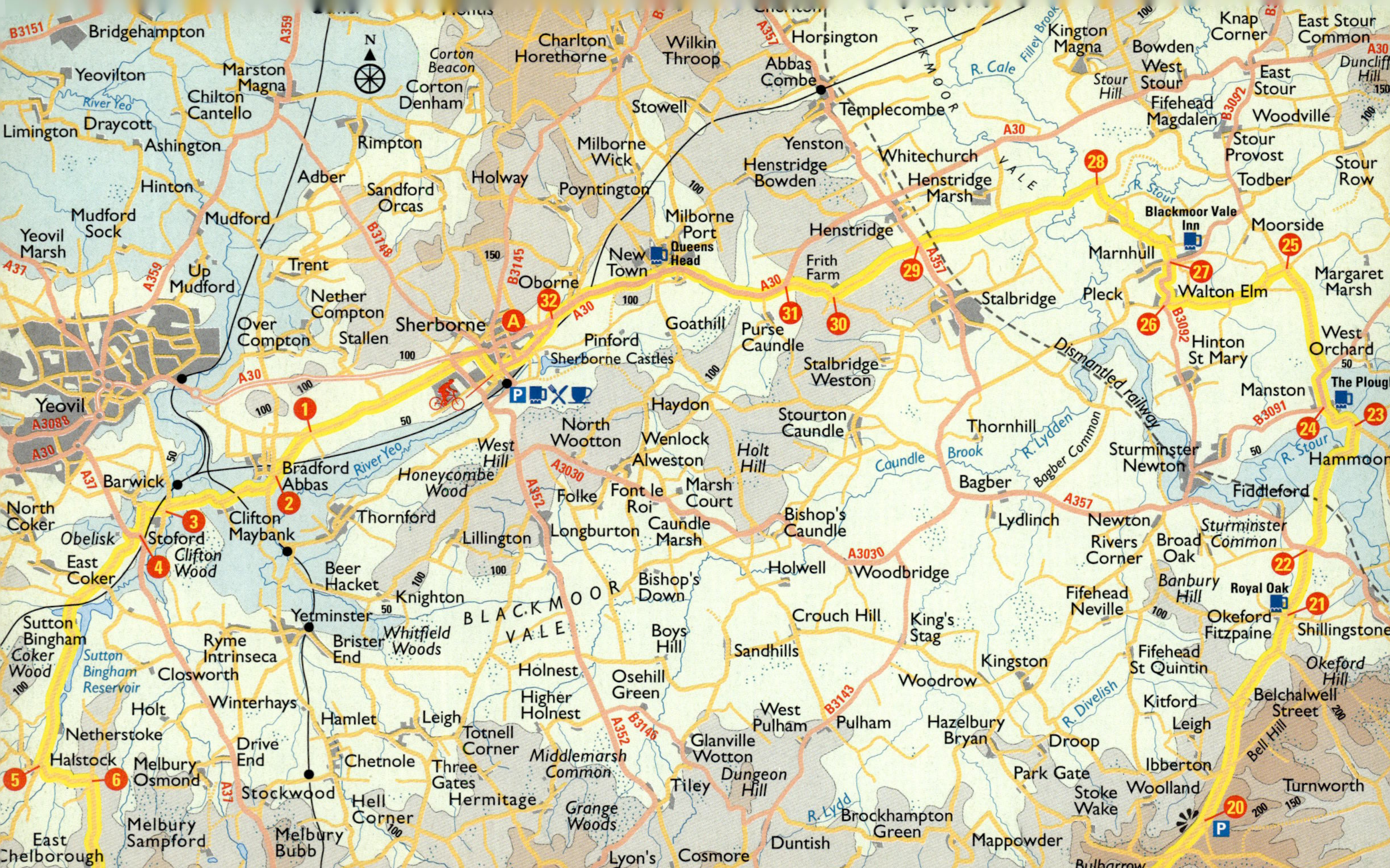

Bridgehampton
Yeovilton
River Yeo
Limington
Draycott
Ashington
Marston Magna
Chilton Cantello
Hinton
Mudford Sock
Yeovil Marsh
Mudford
Up Mudford
Yeovil
Corton Beacon
Corton Denham
Rimpton
Adber
Sandford Orcas
Trent
Nether Compton
Over Compton
Stallen
Sherborne
Charlton Horethorne
Holway
Milborne Wick
Stowell
Wilkin Throop
Poyntington
Milborne Port
New Town
Queens Head
Oborne
Pinford
Sherborne Castles
Goathill
Horsington
Abbas Combe
Templecombe
Yenston
Henstridge Bowden
Henstridge
Frith Farm
Purse Caundle
Stalbridge Weston
Whitechurch
Henstridge Marsh
LACKMOOR
VALE
Stalbridge
R. Cale
Filley Brook
Kington Magna
Stour Hill
Bowden
West Stour
Fifehead Magdalen
Knap Corner
East Stour
East Stour Common
Duncliff Hill
Woodville
Stour Provost
Todber
Stour Row
R. Stour
Blackmoor Vale Inn
Marnhull
Moorside
Margaret Marsh
Walton Elm
Pleck
Hinton St Mary
West Orchard
The Ploug
Manston
Dismantled railway
Thornhill
Brook
R. Lydden
Bagber Common
Sturminster Newton
Hammoon
Fiddleford
Bagber
Caundle
Stourton Caundle
Haydon
North Wootton
West Hill
Wenlock
Alweston
Holt Hill
Honeycombe Wood
Bradford Abbas
Thornford
Folke
Font le Roi
Marsh Court
Lillington
Longburton
Caundle Marsh
Bishop's Caundle
Lydlinch
Newton
Rivers Corner
Broad Oak
Sturminster Common
Barwick
North Coker
Obelisk
Stoford
Clifton Maybank
Clifton Wood
East Coker
Beer Hacket
Knighton
BLACKMOOR
VALE
Bishop's Down
Holwell
Woodbridge
Banbury Hill
Royal Oak
Okeford Fitzpaine
Shillingstone
Fifehead Neville
Yetminster
Whitfield Woods
Brister End
Crouch Hill
King's Stag
Sutton Bingham
Coker Wood
Sutton Bingham Reservoir
Ryme Intrinseca
Closworth
Holnest
Boys Hill
Sandhills
Kingston
Fifehead St Quintin
Okeford Hill
Holt
Winterhays
Higher Holnest
Osehill Green
Woodrow
R. Divelish
Kitford
Belchalwell Street
Netherstoke
Hamlet
Leigh
Totnell Corner
West Pulham
Pulham
Hazelbury Bryan
Leigh
Bell Hill
Halstock
Melbury Osmond
Drive End
Chetnole
Three Gates
Middlemarsh Common
Glanville Wotton
Droop
Ibberton
Stockwood
Hell Corner
Hermitage
Tiley
Dungeon Hill
Park Gate
Woolland
Turnworth
Melbury Sampford
Melbury Bubb
Grange Woods
R. Lydd
Brockhampton Green
Stoke Wake
East Chelborough
Lyon's Gate
Cosmore
Duntish
Mappowder
Bulbarrow
B3151
A359
A37
A3088
A30
B3148
B3145
A357
A3030
A352
B3146
B3143
B3092
B3091
P
N

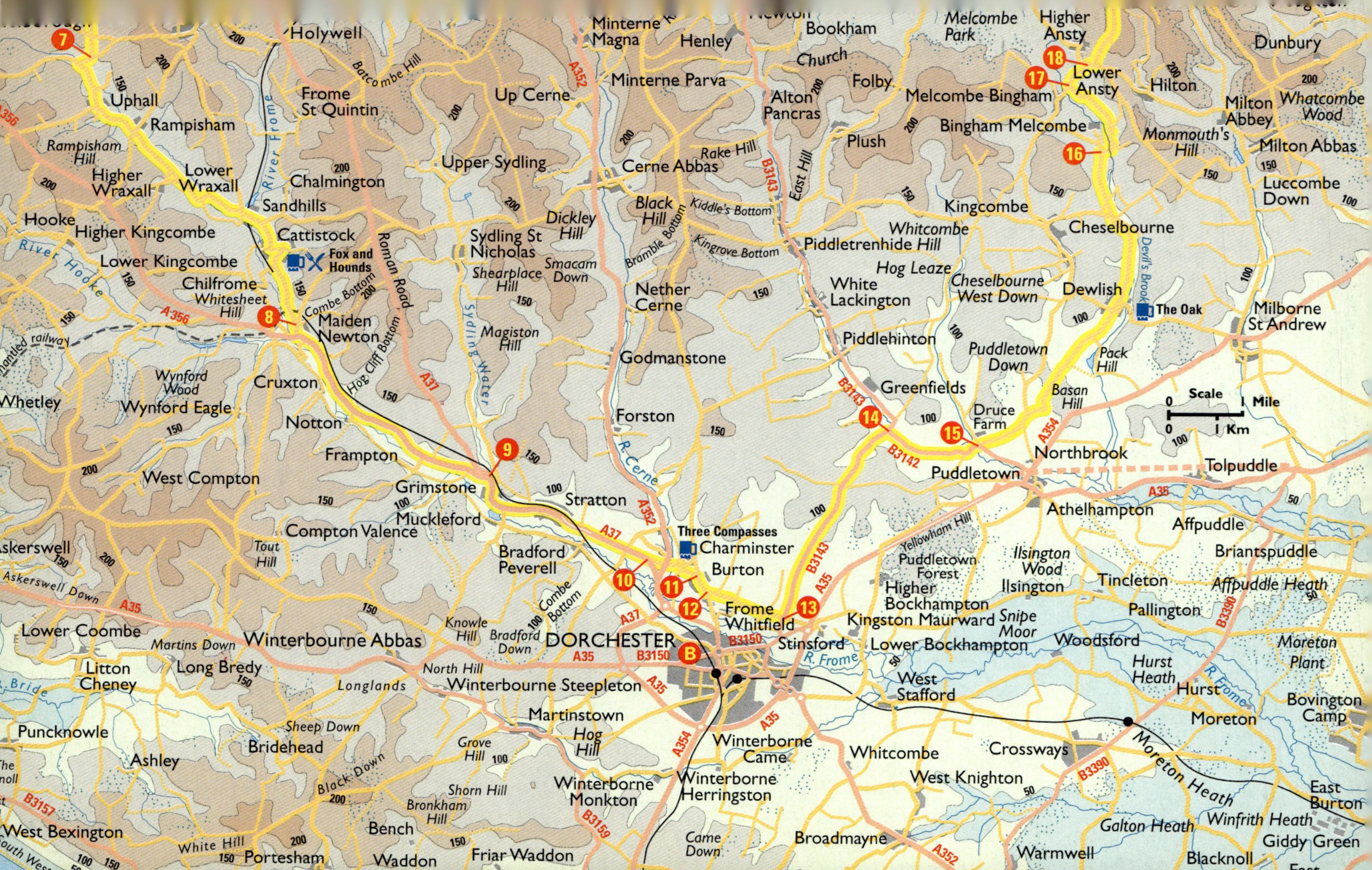

Holywell
Minterne Magna
Henley
Bookham
Melcombe Park
Higher Ansty
Dunbury
Frome St Quintin
Up Cerne
Minterne Parva
Church
Alton Pancras
Folby
Melcombe Bingham
Lower Ansty
Hilton
Milton Abbey
Whatcombe Wood
Uphall
Rampisham
Rampisham Hill
Higher Wraxall
Lower Wraxall
Chalmington
Upper Sydling
Cerne Abbas
Rake Hill
Plush
Bingham Melcombe
Monmouth's Hill
Milton Abbas
Luccombe Down
Hooke
Higher Kingcombe
Sandhills
Cattistock
River Frome
Batcombe Hill
Dickley Hill
Black Hill
Kiddle's Bottom
East Hill
Kingcombe
Cheselbourne
Lower Kingcombe
River Hooke
Fox and Hounds
Roman Road
Sydling St Nicholas
Shearplace Hill
Smacam Down
Bramble Bottom
Kingrove Bottom
Piddletrenhide Hill
Whitcombe
Hog Leaze
Chilfrome
Whitesheet Hill
Combe Bottom
Maiden Newton
Nether Cerne
White Lackington
Cheselbourne West Down
Dewlish
Devil's Brook
The Oak
Milborne St Andrew
dismantled railway
Hog Cliff Bottom
Magiston Hill
Sydling Water
Piddlehinton
Puddletown Down
Pack Hill
Whetley
Wynford Wood
Wynford Eagle
Cruxton
Godmanstone
Greenfields
Druce Farm
Basan Hill
Notton
Forston
R. Cerne
Scale
0
1 Mile
0
1 Km
Frampton
Northbrook
Tolpuddle
West Compton
Grimstone
Stratton
Puddletown
Athelhampton
Affpuddle
Mukleford
Compton Valence
Tout Hill
Three Compasses
Charminster
Yellowham Hill
Puddletown Forest
Ilsington Wood
Briantspuddle
Askerswell
Bradford Peverell
Burton
Higher Bockhampton
Ilsington
Tincleton
Affpuddle Heath
Askerswell Down
Combe Bottom
Frome Whitfield
Kingston Maurward
Snipe Moor
Pallington
Lower Coombe
Knowle Hill
Bradford Down
DORCHESTER
Stinsford
Lower Bockhampton
Woodsford
Moreton Plant
Martins Down
Winterbourne Abbas
Litton Cheney
Long Bredy
North Hill
R. Frome
Hurst Heath
Hurst
Bovington Camp
R. Bride
Longlands
Winterbourne Steepleton
West Stafford
Moreton
Puncknowle
Sheep Down
Martinstown
Bridehead
Hog Hill
Grove Hill
Winterborne Came
Whitcombe
Crossways
Moreton Heath
The Knoll
Ashley
Black Down
Shorn Hill
Winterborne Monkton
Winterborne Herrington
West Knighton
East Burton
Bronkham Hill
Bench
Galton Heath
Winfrith Heath
West Bexington
White Hill
Portesham
Waddon
Friar Waddon
Came Down
Broadmayne
Warmwell
Giddy Green
Blacknoll
South West
A356
A37
A352
B3143
A35
B3142
A354
B3150
B3390
B3159
B3157

Route description

Leave Sherborne by the A30 and then take LHF, SP Bradford Abbas. Cross the A352 and SO to Bradford Abbas.

1 LHF, SP Bradford Abbas.

2 SO, SP Clifton Maybank (where the right turn goes into Bradford Abbas). Then immediately after crossing hump bridge, TR, SP Clifton Maybank.

3 TL, SP Melbury, and almost immediately TR (SP Barwick in the village). Continue under railway and thread round to junction with A37.

4 TR onto A37 (with care) and immediately TL, SP Sutton Bingham (note the obelisk to the right). Continue past Sutton Bingham reservoir.

5 TL, SP Closworth and East Chelborough.

16km (10 miles)

6 TR, SP Rampisham.

7 TR, SP Beaminster, and in 200m, TL, SP Rampisham. Through Rampisham and continue to Cattistock and Maiden Newton.

8 TR, SP Dorchester, and in 300m TL at junction with A356, SP Dorchester.

28km (17.5 miles)

9 TR, SP Dorchester (with care – watch out for fast moving traffic from the left).

Sherborne Abbey

10 LHF, SP Charminster and Herrison. SO crossing A352 and cycle up East Hill.

11 TR, SP Dorchester.

12 TL, SP Frome Whitfield.

42.5km (26.5 miles)

13 To visit Dorchester, TR at next XR and at next TJ, TR onto B3150 and continue into town centre. To continue route, TL at next XR, no SP, onto the B3143 (45km/28 miles).

14 TR, SP Druce.

15 SO at Druce Farm (no SP) on minor road. At each following intersection follow SP Dewlish, continue through village and beyond.

16 TR 4km (2.5 miles) after Dewlish (no SP). The turning is 200m before Bingham Melcombe – easy to miss. This minor road leads through a ford (there is a bridge too) then TL and continue to Ansty.

17 TR, SP Bulbarrow. ***63km (39 miles)***

18 TR then immediately TL, SP Bulbarrow. The route starts to climb!

19 RHF when nearly at top of hill, SP Bulbarrow.

20 SO at top of hill, car park on the right. Freewheel down along the ridge of the hill for the next few kilometres. ***68km (42 miles)***

21 SO by Royal Oak pub, SP Sturminster Newton. ***75km (46.5 miles)***

22 SO over main road, SP Hammoon. SO in Hammoon, by the old stone SP Manston.

23 TL, SP Manston. ***79km (49 miles)***

24 TR, SP Gillingham B3091, and then TL, SP Marnhull.

25 TL, SP Hinton St Mary and Marnhull.

26 TR at sign for Moorside, SP Marnhull.

86km (53.5 miles)

27 SO at XR with B3092 onto narrow road. TL at end into Sodom Lane and TR, SP Marnhull PO. Continue into village. TR by Blackmoor Vale Inn.

28 TL, SP Stalbridge. After 2km (1 mile) where SP indicates Stalbridge Trading Estate, ignore and carry SO.

29 SO, SP Copse House. Long stone wall on your left. ***92km (57 miles)***

30 TR at Frith Farm, no SP.

31 TL at A30, SP Sherborne.

95km (59 miles)

32 TL at Sherborne sign and return to the town centre and the end of the route.

100km (62 miles)

Food and drink

Sherborne has a wide selection of cafés, pubs and restaurants.

Fox and Hounds, Cattistock
Real ales and restaurant.

Three Compasses, Charminster
Bar meals available.

The Oak, Dewlish
Local cyclists campaigned to keep this pub open.

Royal Oak, Okeford Fitzpaine
Local with a beer garden.

The Plough, Manston
Local ales and bar meals.

Blackmoor Vale Inn, Marnhull
Traditional ales. Meals and snacks available. Skittle alley.

Queens Head, Milborne Port
Beer garden. Families welcome.

THE CTC

The CTC is Britain's largest national cycling organisation. Founded in 1878, the CTC has over 65,000 members and affiliates throughout the UK and overseas, and around 200 local groups. The CTC provides essential services for all leisure cyclists, whether you ride on- or off-road, and works to promote cycling and protect cyclists' interests.

CTC membership makes day-to-day cycling easier. A resident expert cycling engineer will answer all your technical queries about cycle buying, maintenance and equipment. And if you get ambitious about your cycling, the CTC's Touring Department has reams of information about cycling anywhere from Avon to Zimbabwe. There is also plenty of practical advice and information in the annual handbook. Then, when it comes to getting kitted out, the shop sells a wide variety of clothing, accessories, books, maps and guide books.

Cycling is good both for you and the environment; it is one of the healthiest activities there is, raising your metabolism, burning fat and toning muscle. However, accidents do happen, and the CTC's membership services mean that when you ride, you are protected by free third party liability of up to £1 million, and by our legal assistance to pursue civil claims.

CTC members also receive *Cycle Touring and Campaigning* magazine free six times a year. *CT&C* takes pride in its journalistic independence. With reports on cycle trips all over the globe, forensic tests on bikes and equipment, and the most vigorous and effective pro-bike campaigning stance anywhere, *CT&C* is required reading for any cyclist.

It is not just members who benefit either: the CTC works on behalf of all Britain's 20 million cycle owners. Its effective campaigning at national level helped to create the Government's National Cycling Strategy. It is lobbying for lower speed limits on country lanes; campaigning so that you can carry bikes on trains; working with local authorities to make towns more cycle-friendly, to ensure that roads are designed to meet cyclists' needs and kept well maintained; making sure that bridleways are kept open; and negotiating cyclists' access to canal towpaths.

Whatever kind of cyclist you are: mountain biker, Sunday potterer, bicycle commuter, or out for the day with your family – cycling is easier and safer with the CTC's knowledge and services in your saddlebag. The CTC is the essential accessory for every cyclist!

For further information contact:
CTC
69 Meadrow
Godalming
Surrey
GU7 3HS

Telephone (01483) 417217
Fax (01483) 426994
e-mail: cycling@ctc.org.uk
Web page: www.ctc.org.uk